D1614857

MISOGYNY ONLINE

SAGE SWIFTS

In 1976 SAGE published a series of short 'university papers', which led to the publication of the QASS series (or the 'little green books' as they became known to researchers). Almost 40 years since the release of the first 'little green book', SAGE is delighted to offer a new series of swift, short and topical pieces in the ever-growing digital environment.

SAGE *Swifts* offer authors a new channel for academic research with the freedom to deliver work outside the conventional length of journal articles. The series aims to give authors speedy access to academic audiences through digital first publication, space to explore ideas thoroughly, yet at a length which can be readily digested, and the quality stamp and reassurance of peer-review.

MISOGYNY ONLINE

A SHORT (AND BRUTISH) HISTORY

EMMA A. JANE

SAGE SWIFTS

Los Angeles | London | New Delhi
Singapore | Washington DC | Melbourne

Los Angeles | London | New Delhi
Singapore | Washington DC | Melbourne

SAGE Publications Ltd
1 Oliver's Yard
55 City Road
London EC1Y 1SP

SAGE Publications Inc.
2455 Teller Road
Thousand Oaks, California 91320

SAGE Publications India Pvt Ltd
B 1/I 1 Mohan Cooperative Industrial Area
Mathura Road
New Delhi 110 044

SAGE Publications Asia-Pacific Pte Ltd
3 Church Street
#10-04 Samsung Hub
Singapore 049483

© Emma A. Jane 2017

First published 2017

Editor: Natalie Aguilera
Editorial assistant: Delayna Spencer
Production editor: Vanessa Harwood
Marketing manager: Sally Ransom
Cover design: Jen Crisp
Typeset by: C&M Digitals (P) Ltd, Chennai, India
Printed and bound by CPI Group (UK) Ltd,
Croydon, CR0 4YY

Library of Congress Control Number: 2016950758

British Library Cataloguing in Publication data

A catalogue record for this book is available from
the British Library

ISBN 978-1-4739-1600-5
eISBN 978-1-4739-2715-5

At SAGE we take sustainability seriously. Most of our products are printed in the UK using FSC papers and boards.
When we print overseas we ensure sustainable papers are used as measured by the PREPS grading system.
We undertake an annual audit to monitor our sustainability.

This book is for all those dudes who *aren't* calling women 'ugly, fat, and slutty' online, and who only send photos of their man parts if a lady or gentleman of the interweb asks very nicely first.

You guys are rad and I love your work.

If R.D. Laing was correct in saying 'few books are forgivable,' then it's surely the case that fewer still are necessary. This book is. Emma Jane has taken some well-worn media and cultural studies orthodoxies and subjected them to a series of trenchant, persuasive, and often laugh-out-loud criticisms. People analysing cybersphere culture and discourse cannot afford to ignore this book.

Chris Fleming, Western Sydney University

Misogyny Online is a rigorous, necessary and at times terrifying exploration of one of the most pressing and rapidly growing forms of harassment and abuse of women and girls today. Dr Jane's interrogation of the rhetoric of sexualised, gendered violence and the rise of multi-perpetrator attacks on individual women using digital technology is a must-read for a greater understanding of this phenomenon and its impact on democracy, culture and the individual.

Tara Moss, author, UNICEF National Ambassador for Child Survival, feminist commentator and human rights advocate.

CONTENTS

ABOUT THE AUTHOR

Emma A. Jane (formerly published as Emma Tom) is an award-winning scholar and author who has been called fat, ugly, and slutty on the internet since the late 1990s. Misogyny online is the focus of her ongoing research into the social and ethical implications of emerging technologies. In 2016, Emma received the Anne Dunn Scholar Award for excellence in research about communication and journalism. This followed her receipt, in 2014, of a Discovery Early Career Researcher Award (DECRA) from the Australian government to fund three years of study into gendered cyberhate and digital citizenship. Emma has presented the findings of her research at the Australian Human Rights Commission, and regularly speaks at large, public events such as the Festival of Dangerous Ideas at the Sydney Opera House. Prior to commencing her academic career, she spent nearly 25 years working in the print, broadcast, and electronic media, during which time she won multiple awards for her writing and investigative reporting. These included the 1997 Henry Lawson Award for Journalism, and the 2001 Women's Electoral Lobby Edna Ryan Humour Award for 'using wit to promote women's interests'. Emma has published eight books including a novel, *Deadset*, which won the Commonwealth Writers' Prize for Asia and the South Pacific for Best First Novel in 1998. Her most recent publication, the fifth edition of *Cultural Studies: Theory and Practice*, was co-authored with Chris Barker and published by SAGE in 2016. Emma is currently a Senior Research Fellow and Senior Lecturer at the University of New South Wales in Sydney, Australia.

ACKNOWLEDGEMENTS

Hello and thank you to my refractory gamerdaughter. Small human, I love you heaps. (Also please stop knowing more than me about internet biz like music.ly and stuff RIGHT THIS MINUTE.) Massive thanks to Melanie Andersen. Your public health brain, hard-arse data crunching, take-no-prisoners critiquing, and cyberhate-free internet experience keep forcing me (in the nicest possible way) to re-think and then re-re-think, again. *Thank you*, Mel. Nicole A Vincent: a big *\o/* for your endlessly generous input into whatever I'm thinking or writing about, but especially into this. (I'm working on a 'Thank you, Nicole' generator to assist with the appreciative gushing, but then I'd need your help with the coding, and then I'd need your help making a second-order generator to thank you properly for the first one, and then ... well, you know how these things end.) Chris Fleming – thinky jukebox and intellectual über dude: I have to exercise restraint here because someone said you wrote something nice for the back of this book. As such, all I'll say is thank you for being the funniest and smartest biped I know, and also for always answering the phone sponsor-style when I need to admit that I am powerless in the face of my irony problem. Nikki Stevens: please refer to the 'gratitude' entry at www.theasuarus.com. Thank you for explaining about the pale ale, for alerting me to all of the things, for all of the checking-ins, and especially for your superlative contrarianism (a description I know you'll say is *all wrong*). Thank you, also: to Jennifer Taylor, Marie-Pierre Cleret, Tara Moss, and Chris Rojek; to my colleagues at the University of New South Wales; and to Delayna Spencer and Natalie Aguilera at SAGE.

The biggest of all the big thank-you(s)-so-much, however, must go to the 50 women who agreed to be interviewed as part of my cyberhate project. I can't believe how much I didn't know before you told me your stories. You guys are ace and I am so very grateful.

Some of the research in this book dates back to the dawn of internet time. Many of the 2.0 bits, however, were researched and written with the support of a Discovery Early Career Research Award (DECRA) from the Australian government. Thank you, Australian government. Bits and pieces of this book have appeared in various forms in papers published in *Feminist Media Studies, Continuum: Journal of Media & Cultural Studies,* the *International Journal of Cultural Studies,* and *Ethics and Information Technology.* Some journalistic versions have also been published in *The Conversation, Daily Life,* and *Medium.*

INTRODUCTION:
THE WARNING
IS YOU WILL RECEIVE
NO WARNING

Men have turned on women online. As a result, the place that was supposed to be radically inclusive – a gender-, race-, and class-free zone – is now delivering female users a blunt message: GTFO. It stands for 'Get The Fuck Out' and is what increasing numbers of women hear when they turn up online. Sometimes the directive is delivered via these four letters alone. More often, however, the messages are embellished:

> You need a good smashing up the arse[1]
>
> sit on a butchers[2] knife so that you may never be able to reproduce[3]
>
> put a toothpick in your vagina, then thrust a wall as hard as you can[4]
>
> fuck off you boring slut … i hope someone slits your throat and cums down your gob[5]
>
> Back to the kitchen, cunt[6]

Perhaps you think the above should have been prefaced with a strong language warning. This, however, is not how it happens for women online. The Australian writer Clementine Ford doesn't receive an official heads-up before the flood of Facebook messages telling her she's a 'feral slut' and 'disgusting hairy lard whale' who should go kill herself, or wither and die from cancer (Ford, 2015). The British activist Caroline Criado-Perez had no forewarning her 2013 campaign to have the Bank of England review its decision to have an all-male line-up on bank notes would provoke tweets such as 'KISS YOUR PUSSY GOODBYE AS WE BREAK IT IRREPARABLY', and 'If your friends survived rape they weren't raped properly' (cited in Criado-Perez, 2013; cited in Philipson, 2013). As for the American gamer and media critic Anita Sarkeesian, she's lost count of the number of times men have used social media to send photos or videos of themselves ejaculating onto her image (Sarkeesian, 2015a). Presumably none of these images contained strategically placed fig leaves or were preceded by 'Not Safe for Work' alerts.

It is, of course, ridiculous to imagine online attackers sending female targets warnings before calling them a 'filthy fucking whore' (cited in Doyle, 2011b) or 'dumb bitch ass cum dumpster' (cited in Jane, 2014b: 566). That would defeat the purpose. To a certain extent it would also be tautology in that many of these messages *are* types of warnings in that they put women on explicit notice that something worse than the message itself is about to happen. When the British Labour MP Stella Creasy supported Criado-Perez, for example, she received a tweet from someone threatening to hack off and eat her breasts (cited in 'If someone walked up and said, "I'm going to rape you", you'd ring 999: Stella Creasy fights the Twitter trolls', 2013). Another read: 'YOU BETTER WATCH YOUR BACK … IM GONNA RAPE YOUR ASS AT 8PM AND PUT THE VIDEO ALL OVER THE INTERNET' (cited in Creasy, 2013). Consider, too, the backlash to journalist Sady Doyle's (2011c) suggestion that gendered harassment has become an inevitable consequence of blogging while female. '**Simply put**,' the men's rights activist Paul Elam responded on his website *A Voice for Men*, '**we are coming for you. All of you**. And by the time we are done you will wax nostalgic over the days when all you had to deal with was someone expressing a desire to fuck you up your shopworn ass' (2011, emphasis in original). Warning? Threat? Either way, these are fighting words.

At this point, a natural question arises: are these graphic articulations of misogynist vitriol an internet phenomenon, or are they the types of things men have always said or thought about women in private? Without a skill set which includes the ability to retrospectively eavesdrop on private conversations, this query is impossible to answer. Many waves of feminist activism and theory do, however, support the contention that while the cyber medium may be new, the 'fuck you up your shopworn ass' message has ample historical precedent. It belongs to a far older tradition of gendered abuse and oppression: one that reduces women to their sexual – or lack of sexual – value and then punishes them for this self-same characterisation. Hot women are just asking for coerced sex because they are hot and leading men on. Women who are not hot enough are just asking for coerced sex because they must be taught a lesson for lacking the obligatory requirement of hotness. As I will show over the course of this book, threats to rape women because of their supposed 'unrapeability' are circulating with astonishing frequency. At the same time men enthuse about wanting to rape certain women as if this is a high compliment.

Given that language offers us endless options for terrorising each other, it is extremely revealing that the rhetoric of sexualised, gendered violence has become so common online. Yet while the internet did not invent sexism, it *is* amplifying it in unprecedented ways. The self-publishing, participatory, and 'share' cultures that are hallmarks of contemporary digital domains mean that men who derogate women have the potential to reach vast audiences of like-minded allies. Under the right conditions, these coalesce into cyber lynch mobs, firing off near identical messages with the relentlessness of profanity-powered machine guns. At the height of the attack against her, Criado-Perez was receiving about 50 rape threats an hour (Battersby, 2013). Over the course of a single weekend, police gathered enough rape and death threats against her to fill 300 A4 pages (Blunden, 2015). In June 2012, Sarkeesian logged more than 100 screen shots of abusive comments over two hours. The latter represented only a fraction of the misogynist harassment she received in response to her attempt to crowd-source funds for a video series about sexism in video games (Sarkeesian, 2012a). During the vicious mob attacks on women in 2014 dubbed 'GamerGate',[7] the games developer Zoë Quinn accumulated 16 gigabytes of abuse (Jason, 2015). In 2016, Jess Phillips – the British Labour MP who helped launch a campaign against misogynist bullying – reported receiving more than 5000 Twitter notifications of people discussing whether or not they would sexually assault her. This included 600 rape threats over the course of a single evening (cited in Oppenheim, 2016).

In many sectors of the internet, graphic rape threats have become a lingua franca – the 'go-to' response for men who disagree with what a woman says, who dislike the way a woman looks, who are unhappy with the response to the unsolicited 'dick pics' they keep sending, or who simply believe, as one commentator recently put it on Facebook, that all women are 'cunts' who deserve to be 'face fucked' until they turn blue (cited in Chalmers, 2015).

Misogyny, in short, has gone viral.[8]

When women speak up about being attacked online, they are frequently instructed to stop complaining and toughen up. 'It's just words,' they are told. 'It's just the internet.' This book, however, shows that gendered hate speech online has significant offline consequences. Female targets suffer socially, psychologically, professionally, financially, and politically. Gendered cyber-hate is having a chilling effect in that some women are self-censoring, writing anonymously or under pseudonyms, or withdrawing partly or completely from the internet. Further, more and more attacks which begin exclusively online are spilling into offline domains. This occurs via practices such as doxing (the publishing of personally identifying information, sometimes to incite internet antagonists to hunt targets in 'real' life), revenge porn (the uploading of sexually explicit material – usually of a former female partner – without the consent of the pictured subject), and – less commonly – swatting (the act of convincing emergency services to storm a target's home by lying about an ongoing critical incident).

When women go to police, the standard response from officers in many jurisdictions is to suggest they simply take a little break from the internet. Women are also being told to use less attractive profile photographs and to engage in less provocative politics online. Such advice is a form of victim blaming and shifts the responsibility for solving the problem of gendered cyberhate to targets. It is also a form of victim punishing, in that women are being told to withdraw from or significantly change their engage-ment within a domain that is widely acknowledged as being an integral and increasingly essential aspect of contemporary life and citizenship (see Mossberger, 2009; Wheeler, 2011; Braman, 2011). The technology writer Nilay Patel (2014) is spot on when he points out that we no longer do things on the internet, we just do things. As such, suggesting that women opt out of the public cybersphere or visit only while wearing the electronic equivalent of propriety-protecting, head-to-toe garments is disenfranchis-ing and entirely unacceptable.

From the infobahn to GamerGate

Much international media coverage is currently being given to the brutality directed at women online, and to the various roles society, law, politics, and corporations (like Facebook and Twitter) should play in formulating responses. Little attention has been paid, however, to the way gendered cyberhate has emerged and evolved over time. This book looks back to the earliest days of the internet to track the history of this new form of old misogyny. Based on nearly two decades of original research, its genealogical approach reveals the unexpected connections and continuities between the counter-cultural idealists whose 'invention' of the internet was underlined by a commitment to egalitarianism, and 'GamerGaters' – members of contemporary gaming communities whose misogyny is so violent, it has been compared to terrorism.[9]

While it is impossible to pinpoint with precision the first time a man made a rape threat against a woman using the internet, in Chapter 1 of this book I show that incidences of gendered cyberhate grew slowly from the late 1990s before spiking around 2010, and then again in 2014 during GamerGate. I offer some insights into the origins of this discourse by outlining my experiences as an early target – and researcher – of such material, as well as showing the way online hostility has morphed and become more prevalent, vitriolic, directly threatening, and gendered over time.

The etiological dimensions of gendered cyberhate are discussed in Chapter 2. While taking care to foreground structural misogyny as the primary explanation for this discourse, this section of the book does examine those aspects of the web's history, design, characteristics, usage patterns, and subcultures which make this medium so conducive to the misogynist message.

The ramifications and consequences of misogyny on the internet are explored in detail in Chapter 3. This chapter outlines the impact of gendered cyberhate on individual targets, larger publics, and broad ideals such as digital inclusivity and gender equity. Philosophical literature on coercion is used to argue that while women who withdraw from the internet to avoid threats and harassment are making a *rational* choice, it is not a *free* choice because they are being coerced into making these changes.

Chapter 4 exposes the way women are consistently blamed for the attacks against them online, while men are routinely excused. The latter often occurs via appeals to motivation, in that it is claimed men are just joking around and do not intend to cause 'real' harm. It is also common for male antagonists to be absented from cyberhate narratives, in that the internet is framed as a place that is inherently dangerous – like Mount Everest during a blizzard – rather than a place that is inhabited by some harm-causing human agents.

Chapter 5 shows that this blame women/excuse men dynamic is also evident in the manifest failures of various institutions to assist targets, bring perpetrators to account, and address the broader problem of gendered violence online. Specifically, it looks at the problematic responses/lack of responses from police, policy-makers, platform operators and corporations, and scholars. With regard to the latter, my argument is that, to a certain extent, some sectors of the academy have been caught off guard by the contemporary epidemic of misogyny online even though this is a phenomenon whose precursory forms have been evident for many years.

In the Conclusion, I discuss potential solutions to gendered cyberhate, and argue that an ethos rooted in the principles of gender equity must guide regulatory – and other – responses going forwards. Specifically, I make the case that while the minutiae of legal and technological changes will vary between jurisdictions and venues, all interventions must involve two commonalities: a willingness to stop blaming female targets, and to start holding male perpetrators accountable for their actions.

Desperately seeking a definition

The phenomenon represented by gendered cyberhate examples such as those furnished at the start of this introduction seems quite stark. It is, however, one that continues to prove difficult to name and define. As I will explain in Chapter 5, heated arguments about what to call heated arguments on the internet have sometimes pulled scholarly focus at the expense of more pressing aspects of the discourse. To cut a long literature review very short, my observations are that when vitriolic or disruptive discourse on the internet has not been coded as being either: a) racist hate speech; or b) cyberbullying affecting children and young people, it has generally been coded as 'flaming' or 'trolling'. When discourse has been coded via either of these terms, it has (at least up until recently) tended to be categorised as some combination of rare, harmless, creative, humorous, important for identity formation, laudably transgressive, aesthetically rich, and so on.

Both 'flaming' and 'trolling' are ambiguous and contested descriptors. The former is somewhat antiquated and usually refers only to heated cyber communications involving invective, insults, negative affect, and so on. 'Trolling', however, is sometimes used to refer to flame-type comments, but is also deployed more specifically to describe the posting of deliberately inflammatory or off-topic material with the aim of provoking responses and emotional reactions in targets. The digital ethnographer Whitney Phillips, meanwhile, strongly rejects the use of 'trolling' as a vague, behavioural catch-all on the internet and uses this term only to describe very specific types of subcultural trolling communities such as those on and around the /b/board in the web forum 4chan (Phillips, 2013, 2015a, 2015c).

Recent scholarly interest in misogyny online has led to the emergence of a range of other expressions used to refer to gendered online hostility, harassment, and abuse. Examples include 'technology violence' (Ostini and Hopkins, 2015), 'technology-facilitated sexual violence' (Henry and Powell, 2015), 'gendertrolling' (Mantilla, 2015), and – from the United Nations (UN) Broadband Commission – 'cyber violence against women and girls' or 'cyber VAWG' ('Cyber violence against women and girls: A world-wide wake-up call', 2015). In this book, I use the terms 'gendered cyberhate', 'gendered e-bile', and 'cyber VAWG' interchangeably to refer to material that is directed at girls or women; that involves abuse, death threats, rape threats, and/or sexually violent rhetoric; and that involves the internet, social media platforms, or communications technology such as mobile telephony (though it may also have offline dimensions). I also use the more colloquial expression 'Rapeglish' to capture the tenor of sexual violence accenting much of this discourse. This book will not attempt to formulate a univocal definition of gendered cyberhate. Rather than engaging in yet another search for a set of objective message characteristics, this book adopts a casuistic approach by providing a multitude of exemplars of gendered cyberhate. A conception of the phenomenon can then be built up by extrapolating from these particulars.[10]

On methods, approaches, and inside information

This book is deliberately personal. The origins of my research are autoethnographic in that I received a great deal of gendered vitriol via the internet while I was working as a journalist and commentator in the Australian print and electronic media. As I will explain over the course of this book, my current scholarly work into misogyny online also means I am targeted for ongoing abuse.

There are advantages to being a researcher who has had first-hand experience of being called ugly, fat, and slutty online. One is that I have been tracking, archiving, and analysing examples of such material since 1998 – well before gendered cyberhate registered on the mainstream media radar or received much attention from scholars. These personal experiences were influential in my choice of PhD topic, and also led to my commencement of a formal study into gendered cyberhate in January 2011. The latter informs this book, and is an ongoing project devoted to mapping and analysing the nature, manifestations, prevalence, etiology, and ramifications of misogyny online, as well as investigating potential remedies. This research is qualitative rather than quantitative, and does not involve representative survey techniques. It is designed, at least in part, to put human faces to the valuable statistical data being collected by other researchers and organisations.

With regard to method, my large archive of gendered cyberhate examples has been assembled using screen shots and web captures, and deploying methodological approaches from the emerging field of internet historiography. Theoretically, my hermeneutic is interdisciplinary and works across feminist and gender theory, legal theory, philosophy, literary studies, and cultural and media studies. Since 2015, a specific aspect of my research – that is, my investigations into the impact of cyberhate on the way women use the internet – has received funding from the Australian government.[11] This book uses the preliminary findings from approximately 50 qualitative interviews conducted as part of this government-funded project. These women – aged between 19 to 52 – were interviewed over the course of 2015 and 2016.[12]

This book has a number of limitations. One is that it utilises emerging findings from research that is ongoing, and which involves terrain in a constant state of flux. My aim, however, is to sketch a genealogy of gendered cyberhate in a manner which remains useful even as its manifestations alter over time. To put it in Foucauldian terms, I hope to offer a 'treatise of intelligibility' which makes various aspects of the current situation intelligible and, therefore, able to be critiqued (Foucault cited in Kritzman, 1988: 101). 'Speaking directly to the present' (Koopman, 2013: 26), in this way, reveals – among other things – the conditions of possibility for the lacklustre institutional responses to the contemporary proliferation of gendered cyberhate in a manner which hopefully paves the way for future action. On a less theoretical note, there is little reason to suppose that the story of gendered cyberhate is likely to ever have a final moment of 'closure'. Given the pressing nature of the problem, therefore, there is good reason to tackle this as an open-ended narrative rather than waiting endlessly for a neat conclusion.

Another limitation of this book is that it focuses on the gendered dimensions of cyberhate as opposed to those aspects of online hate speech which are homophobic, transphobic, racist, culturally intolerant, and so on. This is not to deny or downplay these issues, or the political intersectionality of gender with other social identities. It is simply beyond the scope of this book to explore in any depth the nuances of cyberhate as it relates to race, class, and sexual orientation. On the topic of cultural limitations, I note, too, that while this book does incorporate international statistics, at a qualitative level, its focus is almost entirely anglophone.

Three other potential and probably more provocative limitations of this book are: (1) it does not examine the experiences of women whose internet experiences have been cyberhate free; (2) it does not provide an in-depth examination of men's individual motivations for abusing women online; and (3) it focuses almost exclusively on female targets and male perpetrators. It is not my intention to suggest that all female internet users receive cyberhate, that men's intentions and rationales are of no interest or relevance, or that there exist no female attackers or male targets in the gendered cyberhate scene. That said, my decision-making around these three points is not solely related to project parameters and the tyranny of word-length restrictions.

Firstly, my view is that the clamour for 'balance' in studies of male-perpetrated violence against women (for example, the insistence that such research gives equal space to the voices of women who have *not* experienced gendered violence and of men who are *not* perpetrators) is primarily a diversionary tactic deployed by men's rights activists. Such arguments are on par with the suggestion that research about pedestrian-crossing injuries is incomplete or biased unless equal space is offered to examining the experiences of people who have crossed roads safely, and to airing the views of drivers who have never collided with pedestrians in such circumstances. Unless a project is designed to be explicitly comparative, there is no good reason to acquiesce to these particular demands.

My reasoning in relation to the second of the above points is that, as I will show throughout this book, there has been a focus on the putative motivations of male attackers in a manner which tends to excuse men and to elide the larger problem of gendered cyberhate. Resting this aspect of the phenomenon is a deliberate counter to these trends.

With regards to the third point, that is, the gender of online attackers, I note that several of my interviewees have been attacked savagely by other women and one, a doula and home-birthing activist, has been attacked almost exclusively by other women. While my analysis of this particular manifestation of cyberhate is in its early stages, the data from my interviews suggest that when large groups of women attack other women online, it is often around issues such as pregnancy, parenting, and children's health debates (such as vaccination), as well as debates around, for example, transgender politics, and whether individuals and groups are performing feminism in the 'right' way. While these types of cyberhate do involve gender stereotypes, they are palpably different from the phenomenon addressed in this book and will not be addressed further here.

Focusing primarily on gendered cyberhate involving male attackers and female targets is necessary because of the overwhelming anecdotal and empirical evidence that women are being attacked online more often, more severely, and in far more violently sexualised ways than men. Female targets of cyberhate often receive extremely specific communications about how, where, and even what time they will be violated. Also included may be explicit details about which orifices will be desecrated via which instruments, as well as the names of the family members and children who will be forced to watch. These are not the types of tweets, Facebook messages, and emails typically received by men. Further, the misogyny, sexualised vitriol, slut shaming, and threats women encounter on the internet sit squarely within a much broader problem: namely the grossly high levels of violence that continue to be perpetrated against women and girls around the world ('Cyber violence against women and girls: A world-wide wake-up call', 2015: 13).

With regard to cyberhate directed at men, I note that while the 'ugly, fat, and slutty' trifecta is hurled at women with monotonous regularity, I have yet to witness any men being attacked via this particular combination of insults. While there is an abundance of homophobic slurs and accusations relating to a condition we could call micro-penis syndrome, the low-level argy-bargy experienced by men (or at least by straight, cisgendered, white men) is very different to the abuse experienced by women. Norms do exist around physical appearance for men, but there is no corresponding fixation with men's 'fuckability' or 'rapeability'. This reflects the broader fact that men are not traditionally shamed for promiscuity or sexualised self-representation. There is still no male version of the word 'slut' – or at least not one with derogatory connotations.

When the rhetoric of sexual violence *is* used to abuse men online, it is often delivered via attacks on their female partners and family members (Jane, 2014b: 565). In 2011, for instance, an attack on the former US television talk show host Jon Stewart included the posting of photographs of his wife alongside disparaging comments about her size and attractiveness. These included: 'Most lib's chicks are pigs', 'She a liberal. They only come in ugly', and 'Looks like a trip to Auschwitz might do her some good' (comments beneath 'Jon Stewart's wife Tracey is overweight, unattractive', 2011). Another example is the case of the Australian footballer Robbie Farah who, following the death of his mother, received a tweet reading: 'I'd still fuck your mum, I will have to wear a gas mask to help with the smell of decomposing flesh, but I'd fuck her hard' (@maxpower118 cited in Thomson, 2012). In 2016, Ken Kratz, the widely disliked American prosecutor from the Netflix docu-series *Making a Murderer*, reported receiving messages from people saying they hoped his daughter would be raped in front of him (cited in Bacchiocchi, 2016). In the same year, explicitly worded rape threats were tweeted about the one-year-old daughter of the English footballer Jamie Vardy (Oliphant, 2016). These examples show that violent misogyny can still be present in cyberhate attacks in which men are the primary targets.

Before moving away from the topic of this book's potential limitations and towards the more pleasant (at least from my perspective) subject of its potential merits, I wish to return to the issue of my first-hand experience of and personal involvement with its subject matter. My current cyberhate study has resulted in some criticism from people identifying as pro-GamerGate that my research should not be trusted because I am biased.[13] I am happy to own those definitional aspects of bias relating to an 'inclination, a propensity, [and] a predisposition' (Brown, 1993: 2333). My study of misogyny online is undoubtedly driven by pre-existing curiosity arising from my own experience. I suspect this is not unusual in academia. Research programs are often long and gruelling to the point where a degree of personal investment may well be required in order to bring even modest projects to completion. (And even then, it is not uncommon to hear the scholarly equivalent of 'are we there yet?' as per the back seat lament from children during long car trips.) My first-hand experience of gendered cyberhate has indeed sustained my interest in the subject over many years. Without this personal experience, I would not have assembled such a large archive, obtained so many valuable prototypical examples, or spent nearly two decades looking out for, collecting, and thinking about such material. Yet does this personal connection mean my work is inevitably tainted by selection and confirmation bias? After much agitation about this question, my considered answer is, 'it depends'.

Accusations of bias raise a plethora of interesting issues, including some perennial questions concerning the relationship between certain kinds of distance and knowledge.[14] Imagine I ask you a question about your partner, and then, after you answer (perhaps in a way I do not like), I tell you I've decided my query was ill-conceived because you are in an intimate relationship with this person and are therefore partisan. On one hand, I am correct. You cannot possibly be objective. On the other hand, your intimate acquaintance with the subject gives you access to a wealth of inside information which makes you perfectly placed to answer such questions. This demonstrates the way 'insider' and 'outsider' forms of knowledge both have advantages and liabilities. Certainly, those who are involved and/or invested in a topic may understand the 'grammar' of an issue in a deeper way than those who are unengaged or uninvolved. Consider the philosopher René Girard whose work is predicated on what could be called 'the epistemology of the victim' (C. Fleming, personal communication, 2015). That is, the victim – or the perspective of the victim – can tell us things about our culture that the victimiser cannot.

This view will obviously be unsatisfactory to those who subscribe to an epistemology of realism which maintains that a sufficiently rigorous researcher is able to occupy an Archimedean vantage point offering unmediated and absolutely objective access to the world. For me, however, the issue at stake is not whether a scholar's experience of an object of analysis endangers their objectivity (because my view is that this is epistemically unavoidable); it is whether a researcher owns up to their inevitable lack of objectivity and offers as much information as possible about how their subjectivism might manifest. Indeed, critics who accuse others of a lack of objectivity may well be failing to acknowledge their own standpoints.

When I think back to the first rapey emails I received in the late 1990s, to the best of my recollection, my thought processes went something along the lines of: 'Huh. How very weird, interesting, and creepy. I wonder what all this is about?' This is opposed to, say, a thought process more along the lines of: 'Ah ha! Finally, some proof of a view I happened to have held before I had any actual proof!' Once I developed a modest working thesis ('there seems to be a bit of misogyny on the internet'), I endeavoured to seek out, examine, and give adequate consideration to material which contradicted or was otherwise a poor fit for this thesis. Over the years, however, I have found an abundance of evidence to support my early thesis and very little data suggesting it requires diluting or reversing. As it happens, my current thesis is even more strongly worded than my first. It is: 'there seems to be a *lot* of misogyny on the internet and a great deal of it involves sexually explicit threats of violence.'

These claims I am making about the virtues of my research approaches are unlikely to surprise. *Obviously* I would say I have conducted my inquiries in as fair-minded a fashion as possible. It would be most peculiar to start a book warning that one's work ought not to be trusted because one is a prejudiced polemicist. What I will endeavour to do, however, is to be as transparent as possible about the way I have conducted my research and reached my conclusions, and leave it to you, the reader, to make your own decisions about the rigour of my methods and the validity of my claims. To a certain extent, the inclusion of first-person material in this book is to assist you in deciding whether my personal experiences are likely to constitute a help or a hindrance to my research. Mostly, however, I cite my own email in-box because I suspect that you, like me, will be gob smacked to observe that the rape-a-rific emails sent to a rowdy, sex-positive newspaper columnist in the late 1990s are all but identical to those sent to a devout Catholic blogger on the other side of the world more than a decade later.

'holy shit you dumb bitch I'm unloading my whole nutsack on your face'

This book began with a warning about lack of warnings. I wanted readers unfamiliar with gendered cyberhate to get a sense of what it's like to be suddenly yelled at in Rapeglish. In the meantime, I note that while female cyberhate targets may not receive official warnings before the arrival of graphic and garishly punctuated threats to dismember and penetrate their bodies, gendered cyberhate has become normalised to the extent that many have come to expect it. Especially if they speak out about how they have come to expect it. For years now, Sarkeesian has been attacked so relentlessly she has had to cancel speaking engagements and use private security

(Marcetic, 2014; Goddard, 2015: 6). At the height of GamerGate in 2014, she also had to leave her home. Yet the feminist games commentator doggedly continues to detail the deluge of abuse she receives despite knowing full well that talking about online harassment invariably generates more of it. In late 2015, for instance, she posted a series of tweets describing the aforementioned ejaculation images as some of the most disturbing and vile sexual harassment she had ever received (Sarkeesian, 2015a). The ugly truth, she wrote, is that male harassers are weaponising their genitalia and sexuality 'as a way of trying to disempower and keep women in line' (2015a). Many men disagreed. They prosecuted their case that there is no misogyny on the internet via tweets such as:

> This fucking account makes me want to bash women and I consider myself pretty level headed (Ciroc Obama);
>
> I've never came on a girls avi[15] before but holy shit you dumb bitch I'm unloading my whole nutsack on your face ($LATER); and
>
> STOP COMPLAINING YEEEE BLOODY CUNT. (william)

The self-performative contradiction (a polite, academic term for 'rampant hypocrisy') is truly astounding. As is the gendered violence of the rhetoric. To adequately convey the nature and force of contemporary misogyny online, I believe it is necessary not only to cite a multitude of examples, but to cite a multitude of *unexpurgated* examples.[16] Indeed, as I will argue in Chapter 5, the metaphorical unspeakability of gendered cyberhate may be one of the reasons it has become as prevalent as it has. In scholarship, especially, it has tended to be referred to via generic descriptors such as 'hostile', 'graphic', 'in bad taste', and so on. Yet these euphemisms fail to capture the toxic misogyny in play. Compare the difference between the following:

1. Women are receiving sexually explicit rape threats online.
2. Women are receiving sexually explicit rape threats online such as, 'I will fuck your ass to death you filthy fucking whore. Your only worth on this planet is as a warm hole to stick my cock in'.[17]

To fully grasp the nature and extent of the problem, we must bring it into the daylight and look at it directly, no matter how unsettling or unpleasant the experience might be.

So, let us steel ourselves and begin.

Notes

1   This was sent as a tweet to Criado-Perez in 2013 (cited in Criado-Perez, 2013).
2   I will not be writing 'sic' after presentation errors in material cited from the internet in recognition of the informality of these contexts. I will also be spelling expletives out in full in those situations where I am aware that media outlets have replaced certain letters with hyphens, asterisks, and so on.
3   This was part of a Facebook message sent to Ford in 2015 (cited in Harris, 2015).
4   This was tweeted at the Australian activist Coralie Alison in 2015 (cited in Hernandez, 2015).
5   This was sent to the US tech expert Kathy Sierra in 2007 (cited in Walsh, 2007).
6   This was sent to Sarkeesian in 2012 (TheDaveKD cited in Sarkeesian, 2012a).
7   As with my use of terms such as 'feminism', my use of 'GamerGate' in this book is not to imply that this is a homogenous movement.
8   I first used this phrase in a media interview on 30 July 2015 http://www.dailytelegraph.com.au/news/nsw/why-do-men-threaten-women-with-rape-to-shut-them-up-on-the-web/news-story/0abd8403e59747a51717f54b81a21b46). At the same time a book by Karla Mantilla was published with the phrase in its subtitle, *Gender Trolling: How Misogyny Went Viral.*
9   See Marcetic, 2014; Cooper, 2014; Lee, 2014; Thériault, 2015.
10 For a more detailed discussion of this approach see Jane, 2014a, 2014b.
11 This is in the form of a Discovery Early Career Researcher Award (DECRA) which is funding a three-year project called 'Cyberhate: The new digital divide?'.
12 Two groups of interviewees were recruited via a number of methods, including: advertising on online and offline fora; direct personal approaches; and chain-referral sampling. The first group comprise Australian women with a public profile who have experienced hostility or threats online, and who have spoken about this previously in a public forum. These women had the option of being identified using their real names in research outputs, and most made use of this option. The second group comprise women who are not in public life and who have experienced hostility or threats online but have not spoken about this previously in a public forum. These interviewees all used pseudonyms and all identifying details were removed from their transcripts. While my recruitment techniques were not designed to obtain a representative population sample, I did ensure that my interview cohort included women of colour, queer women, and Muslim women, as well as women from a range of ages and socio-economic circumstances. Throughout this book I will indicate which subjects were interviewed by me as part of my research project, and also when pseudonyms are being used.
13 See Rahman, 2015; Ankucic, 2015.
14 Many thanks to Chris Fleming for input into this section.
15 My understanding of 'avi' here is that it refers to 'avatar', that is, a symbol, figure, or image used to represent a human player in a game or other computer-mediated environment.
16 For a more detailed version of this argument see Jane, 2014b.
17 This was tweeted at the feminist writer Sady Doyle (cited in Doyle, 2011b).

I

THE RISE OF RAPEGLISH

'Congratulations on your white penis'

> For years, it's been an open secret that having a visibly female online identity – especially if one writes about sexism – is a personal security risk. (Doyle, 2011c)

> Being harassed on the internet is such a normal, common part of my life that I'm always surprised when other people find it surprising. You're telling me you don't have hundreds of men popping into your cubicle in the accounting department of your mid-sized, regional dry-goods distributor to inform you that – hmm – you're too fat to rape, but perhaps they'll saw you up with an electric knife? No? Just me? People who don't spend much time on the internet are invariably shocked to discover the barbarism – the eager abandonment of the social contract – that so many of us face simply for doing our jobs. (L West, 2015)

> If you're thinking, 'Well come on that doesn't seem like that big a problem,' well congratulations on your white penis. Because if you have one of those, you probably have a very different experience on the Internet. (Jon Oliver cited in Roy, 2015)

If you're not being called ugly, fat, and slutty on the internet, odds are you're a man. Or a woman pretending to be a man. This is not hyperbole. In 2015, the UN Broadband Commission released a report citing research showing that 73 per cent of women and girls have been exposed to or have experienced some form of online violence ('Cyber violence against women and girls: A world-wide wake-up call', 2015: 2). The report acknowledges: that women are 27 times more likely to be abused online than men; that 61 per cent of online harassers are male; and that women aged between 18 and 24 are at particular risk (p. 15). These international figures comport with data collected in individual countries. For example, a survey of 3000 Australians aged 18 to 54 reveals that one in five women overall and two in five women aged 18 to 19 report having been targeted for digital sexual harassment (Powell and Henry, 2015a: 1–2). While women and men in Australia are equally likely to report experiencing digital harassment and abuse, women are more likely to report *sexual* harassment, are significantly more likely to be 'very or extremely upset' by the abuse, and are more likely to take actions such as changing their online details or profile settings, or leaving a site (Powell and Henry, 2015a: 1). Similarly, a 2014 study by the Pew Research Center in the United States reports that men are more likely to experience name-calling and embarrassment – harassment of the types categorised as less severe: 'a layer of annoyance so common that those who see or experience it say they often ignore it' (Duggan, 2014: 2–3). Young women, in contrast, are particularly vulnerable to severe types of abuse such as stalking, and sexual harassment (p. 3). University of Maryland researchers, meanwhile, have found that internet accounts with feminine usernames incur an average of 100 sexually explicit or threatening messages for every four received by male users (Citron, 2014a: 14).

The problem is particularly acute for women in the media. In 2016, *The Guardian* engaged in a quantitative analysis of its own comment threads and – after examining 70 million remarks – found that of the 10 regular writers who received the most abuse, eight were women (four white and four non-white) while two were men of colour (Gardiner et al., 2016). The 10 regular writers who received the least abuse were all men. Since 2010, journalism produced by female contributors has consistently attracted more comments requiring blocking by *The Guardian*'s moderators, with articles about feminism and rape attracting very high levels of blocked comments (as opposed to comments on articles about crosswords, cricket, horse racing, and jazz, which tend to be 'respectful') (Gardiner et al., 2016). The largest number of objectionable comments targeted Jessica Valenti, the feminist writer and founder of the blog *Feministing* (Valenti, 2016). Similar trends have been observed in Australia, where a 2016 survey by the Women in Media group found that 41 per cent of female journalists were being harassed, bullied, or trolled online ('Australian media still a Blokesworld in 2016', 2016).

As for the throwaway line about women using the internet in drag, the American legal scholar Danielle Keats Citron cites a study of multiplayer online gamers suggesting that 70 per cent of females play as male characters to avoid sexual harassment (2014a: 18). (This is not an insubstantial number given that – despite the widely held belief that most gamers are male – statistics from the Pew Research Center show that equal numbers of women and men now play video games (Duggan, 2015).) In 2015, the writer Alex Blank Millard engaged in her own gender-swap experiment to highlight the misogynist nature of online abuse. Sick of constantly receiving rape threats from 'faceless eggs' online, she changed her Twitter profile photo to that of a white man – but kept the content she posted the same. When Millard tweeted about rape culture, fat shaming, and systemic oppression as Lady Alex, the standard response was a deluge of rape and death threats, and a bunch of guys calling her fat. When she commented on the same things as Straight- and Cis-Looking White Dude Alex, she was retweeted, favourited, and even cited by Buzzfeed (Millard, 2015).

Misogyny online has become so pervasive and has received so much media coverage that it can be difficult to remember a time when the internet didn't seem to be made out of rape threats. In this chapter, I offer some early examples of e-bile to show that this discourse did not suddenly appear in recent years, but has a back story pre-dating social media. Tracking the history of gendered cyberhate also reveals the way the problem has changed from being one that is experienced by only a few women via only a few channels, to one that is experienced by many women via multiple platforms. This helps explain how we have reached the point where dodging rape threats online is 'a daily obstacle course' for women (Gold, 2013); where 'any woman who makes the mistake of having a thought in her mind, and then vocalizing it online' risks horrendous abuse (Oliver cited in Roy, 2015); and where being called 'a fucking disgusting feminist piece of shit, stupid shark mouth with ugly tits' (Cranston, 2015) is simply the cost of using the internet while possessing (or appearing to possess) a vagina.

'You look like a tart desperate for cock' – close encounters with retro Rapeglish

I have been archiving rapey emails since 1998. Back then I didn't realise rapey messages were going to become a thing and I didn't call it 'archiving'. Back then, it was more a case of keeping all the X-rated hate mail that arrived on my computer, just in case… In case of *what*, I wasn't entirely sure.

But when strangers suddenly start sending computerised messages addressed to 'You Fucking Arsie Cunt', it makes an impression.

In 1998, I had been a journalist for a decade, and was accustomed to receiving strongly worded snail mail from readers who objected to my sex-positive, third-wave feminist commentary. Some said they had written to my editors threatening to suspend their newspaper subscriptions until they received proof I had been sacked. A retired senior naval officer (who pointed out that he'd had 'plenty of overseas experience, including embassy duties') accused me – in perfect penmanship – of espousing unbridled licentiousness. Someone else said my work 'read like some nightmare of verbal pollution'. A self-described 'Royalist and Anglo Saxon Protestant' signed off a letter with 'No Regards to you', before explaining that he was off to his Uniting Church to order 'another copy picture of her Royal Highness photo' because he felt despoiled after exposure to my articles. Over the years, I was also called a 'Pretend Journalist', a member of the 'Jew-media-intellectual-dictatorship', and both 'sick' and in need of 'an psychiatrist' (emphases in originals). The take-away point here is that while many readers disliked me and my work very much, not once did any of them ever propose corrective gang rape as an intervention.

All this changed in 1998 when – like many other crazy-naïve print media columnists – I began including my new-fangled email address at the end of my work on the off chance readers felt motivated to engage. Readers did. Here is a representative sample of the type of message that began flooding my inbox on a weekly, daily, and sometimes hourly basis:

> What is your agenda? 'Girl power?' To hate men? Or just being your stupid self? You should have a good arse fuck lasting two hours every day. That would set you right! You look like a tart desperate for cock or maybe you think you're cool or funky? All feminists should be gangraped to set them right. Plus work in a hore house for a year or so. Women had never had voting right thru history of man-kind. And should not have it now either.

Also:

> your article reeks of a half ugly lesbian, determined to get her own back on all the men who refused to fuck her over all these years. We all know that for $35 a bloke can get a full body massage, his dick wanked for him, by a pretty little 18 year old, not some sad assed thing like you with a hatred of men.

Emails like this were not rare. On the days my column was published, they arrived faster than I could keep up with them. And I wanted to keep up with them. Despite – but also *because* of – the 'ewww' factor, they were intriguing. The imagery was so starkly different from anything I had ever received previously. Yes, I was used to *ad hominem* attacks. Sure, I knew many detractors objected not only to my politics but to the fact that I had a job in journalism at all. Yet even the angriest 'sack her now!' letters were extremely polite. The graphic, sexualised language, and the threatening undertones in the emails, was entirely new. I'd never seen anything like it in readers' letters before. Quite frankly, I'd never seen anything like it *anywhere* before. I wondered what kind of person talked like this. What kind of person read through a newspaper and thought: 'Hmmm. I don't appreciate Reporter X's writing. I think I'll send some hard-core porn-mail recommending a good, solid raping. Now there's a response that's both appropriate and proportionate!' Except that I wasn't Reporter X. I was *Girl* Reporter X. I began asking my male peers whether they were receiving emails from disgruntled female readers threatening pack sodomy, de-testiclisation, and wall-to-wall sexual violence.

They said, 'no'.

Looking back, I don't think the arrival of Rapeglish into my home office in 1998 had that much to do with me or the cultural conditions of the late 1990s at all. Rather, the combination of disgust and desire expressed by those male correspondents seemed to speak to something far older about men's attitudes to women, to female sexuality, and to actual or perceived female power. While the advent of email allowed these sentiments to be expressed with ease and anonymity, it did not create them.

At the time, however, I couldn't help wondering whether the reason I was receiving so much Rapeglish was because of what I was writing or the way I was writing it. While it went against all my feminist principles, I couldn't help wondering whether I'd brought all this on myself, whether somehow I was asking for it.

'She gave great blowjobs before her fall, now imagine the pleasure she will bring with out her front teeth' – cyberhating on cheerleaders

In 2006, I had completed a master's program around full-time freelance work in journalism. I had also been diagnosed with a surprise pregnancy and made the (in retrospect slightly insane) decision to start a PhD. My interest in the disgust/desire/disavowal dynamic epitomised by comments like 'you should be raped for being so grossly unrapeable' was extremely influential on the direction of my doctoral research. My thesis looked at the fetishistic way cheerleaders are talked about and represented in popular culture, the news media, online domains, and pornography. I was particularly fascinated at how cheerleaders were routinely dismissed as slutty bimbos unworthy of anyone's attention, while simultaneously being paid a great deal of attention indeed. Rhetorically, there were also strong similarities between the 'half ugly lesbian' messages I was continuing to receive and the comments circulating about cheerleaders in various male-dominated internet fora. Like my burgeoning collection of electronic hate mail, cyber-hating on cheerleaders often involved hyperbolic and sexualised vitriol, as well as a kind of lascivious contempt. Thus targets – including high school-aged girl targets – were hypersexualised as 'sluts', and then derogated for being 'sluts' who did not pass muster because they were too ugly, too fat, too small breasted, too old, too lesbian, and so on.[1] Violent and coercive sex was then prescribed as reward for those cheerleaders deemed worthy, and as punishment and rehabilitation for those who were not.

A significant difference between the material being sent to me and the comments I observed circulating about cheerleaders concerned the way the medium was beginning to shape the contours of the message. While emails sent to my private address were a one-to-one form of communication, the stichomythic banter permitted in public fora online was resulting in a 'gamification' of the abuse, in that participants appeared to be competing to see who could generate the most creative and offensive derision. Consider the following group discussion about a cheerleading photograph posted on an Australian video game site in 2009. The initial poster observes that there are a 'couple of nice blondes in this pack' (paveway commenting beneath 'NRL cheerleaders to go?', 2009). This prompts:

After seeing that fatty at the front.. BAN CHEERLEADERS! (TicMan);

I see a muffin top. Repeat muffin top! Send backup! (darkjedi);

hahaha ticman, yeah she's a f——g mong hey her face is f——-g weird like a downy or something (paveway); and

I go to the football to watch footy, not watch some fat trogs whos faces resemble a bucket of smashed crabs (casa).

Similarly intensifying abuse can be observed in response to amateur footage of a high school cheerleader falling from a human pyramid posted on a website called *Nothing Toxic*. One person says it is OK that this girl has fallen because she is used to 'bouncing her face on Wood'[2] (Killerdude commenting on 'Cheerleader falls on her face in front of the school', 2008). Subsequent remarks include: 'Haha stupid cunt' (Pubikare); 'watching a cheerleader get owned[3] is only topped by watching one get anal' (spazemunky); 'Odd that she was splitting her minge lips for the audience one second then splitting her other lips on the floor the next' (markels65), and – perhaps the 'winning' entry in this bout of citizen shock jockery – 'She gave great blowjobs before her fall, now imagine the pleasure she will bring with out her front teeth' (Yellaa_Fella).

The exchange on *Nothing Toxic* demonstrates the way key characteristics of gendered cyberhate such as explicit sexual references, themes of violence and coercion, schadenfreude, and the contempt/desire paradox are amplified by group dynamics. As participants vie to trash their target in the most over-the-top manner possible, they stand to accrue various benefits such as those associated with in-group cohesion, scapegoating, and taboo humour. As prosaic as the observation may seem, they also seem to be having *fun*. This sort of 'hateplay', 'signviolence', and 'recreational nastiness' (Jane, 2014a: 531–2) has become a key mode of engagement in internet contexts and one that has been discussed – and often defended – in relation to the activities of subcultural trolling communities. This raises the loaded issue of hate speech and intent: that is, whether speech which appears to be hateful can still be classified as hateful if a speaker's avowed or putative intention is something other than hate. My case, made in more detail in Chapter 4, is that it is entirely possible for a person to produce hate speech even if they claim their primary intention is, for example, to have fun, ward off boredom, satirise hate speech, and so on.

'I endured too many references to "cum" – canaries and coal mines'

By the end of 2010, I had a mostly completed PhD, a four-year-old daughter, and a draft copy of a new *résumé* I hoped would lead my employment prospects away from the print media (an industry which seemed to be heading towards buggy whip oblivion) and towards full-time academic work. By this stage, I had also assembled a sizable archive of cyberhate directed: (a) at me;

(b) at cheerleaders; and (c) at targets who were neither members of (a) nor (b). Looking around the cybersphere, it had become clear that being called ugly, fat, and slutty online no longer meant one was part of an exclusive club. One of many things that were not clear, however, was how widespread this gendered cyberhate thing was becoming. My post-doctoral research attempted to answer this and other questions.

There are few public self-reports of gendered cyberhate from the late 1990s to around 2010. This raises the question of whether such discourse was relatively rare during the early decades of the internet, or whether it was present but not discussed. In Chapter 3, I show that many targets of misogyny online are indeed reluctant to talk – at least in an identifiable way – about some aspects of their experiences. That said, the mainstream uptake of feminist ideals in the West since the 1970s makes it difficult to imagine that large numbers of women were receiving such material and remaining mute. (I, for instance, wrote my first newspaper article about the subject in 2002.) My conclusion, therefore, is that the gendered, sexually explicit, and threatening dimensions of contemporary cyberhate – as well as its extraordinary prevalence – are relatively new.

There are, however, a handful of reports of gendered cyberhate that did occur during these early years. A particularly vicious example, in mid-2006, involved a group of Australian teenage boys who filmed the sexual assault of a teenage girl, before selling the video at schools and then on the internet (Henry and Powell, 2015: 758). The footage depicted the boys urinating on the girl, setting her hair on fire, and forcing her to participate in sex acts. Another example, from 2008, involved an American student who was subjected to ongoing cyberhate including public posts advising men to wear two condoms before anally raping her because she had untreated herpes (cited in Citron, 2014a: 1–2). The attacks on this woman were so relentless and so numerous that, at one point, 75 per cent of the links appearing on the first page of a search of her name were made up of abuse sites and disparaging posts. These said – among much else – that she was a 'stupid slut' who enjoyed rape and rough sex and who had been fired from jobs because of 'sexual misconduct' (2014a: 2–3).

Female journalists also began reporting stories similar to my own in that they said they were used to receiving angry correspondence by snail mail, but had noticed a stark difference in the type and volume of material that arrived once their work shifted onto internet platforms. Joan Walsh (2007), the former editor-in-chief of *Salon*, says that, as a columnist for the print media, she was well accustomed to 'nasty letter-writing campaigns'. Like me, however, she began receiving a very different type of correspondence after commencing web-based commentary in 1998:

> I'd never been truly, viciously attacked, in terms relating to my intellect, my appearance or my sexuality, and I'd never experienced a personal threat … But once I joined *Salon* I started receiving the creepiest personal e-mails about my work … I endured too many references to 'cum' in those e-mails. I'll forgo other details for the sake of brevity and discretion. (Walsh, 2007)

As previously stated, I do not agree it is wise to forego these 'other details' for reasons of brevity or discretion. Walsh (2007) would also prove to be incorrect in her prediction that, while women did have it harder than men online, misogynist trolls constituted only 'a tiny sliver of the Web population'. Gendered cyberhate was a growth rather than a niche market, and these few, early examples were portents of the pandemic to come. As Kathy Sierra (2014), the woman who was about to become gendered cyberhate's first big name target, recalls of the first online threat she received in 2004: 'I thought it was a one-off, then. Just one angry guy. And it wasn't really THAT bad. But looking back, it was the canary in the coal mine …'.

Before moving on to more contemporary iterations of gendered hate speech in the online coal mine, I offer the following textbox to highlight some features of the prototypical examples discussed above. These also show the emergence of some attributes that have become signal characteristics of the discourse so prevalent today. Note that this textbox is designed to illustrate general trends rather than to offer a rigid matrix. Just as the 2006 sexual assault case from Australia does not fit neatly into this grid, there are bound to be other cases which have similarly exceptional elements.

GENDERED CYBERHATE PRIOR TO 2010

EARLY TARGETS

- Are female or female-identifying online;
- Are in some way visible in the public sphere/public cybersphere;
- Have achieved a degree of success in their chosen field, have a fan-base, and/or have access to an audience;

- Are openly opinionated;
- Perform, foreground, or are perceived as performing or foregrounding themes of sex or sexuality; and/or
- Hold feminist views.

EARLY ATTACKERS

- Are male or male-identifying online; and/or
- Are anonymous, quasi-anonymous,[4] or otherwise difficult to identify.

EARLY DISCOURSE

- Passes caustic judgment on women's appearance or sexual attractiveness – often expressed in terms not only of their 'fuckability' but their 'rapeability';
- Deploys *ad hominem* invective;
- Includes hyperbolic misogyny, homophobia, and/or sexually graphic imagery;
- Prescribes coerced sex acts as all-purpose correctives; and/or
- Involves disavowal in that authors fixate on their targets while insisting explicitly or implicitly that nothing about their targets is worthy of notice.

'Shut the fuck up you fucking ugly OLD wowser cunt' – outing the internet as misogynist

Sierra was right about the canary. In March of 2007, she was subjected to an extraordinary attack. It was one marking the beginning of the shift from misogyny online that was contained, unplanned, and low-profile, to that which was viral, quasi-coordinated, and eminently visible.

At the time, Sierra was one of the most high-profile women in tech (Sandoval, 2013). Trolls declared 'open season' on the software designer after she said something they found unforgivable. And what was the statement so egregious it incited an online savaging? Sierra had had the hide to say that while she didn't moderate comments on her own blog, she supported those who did (Sierra, 2014). In contemporary contexts, it is common and relatively uncontroversial knowledge that hate speech proliferates in the below-the-line comment sections of websites. In 2016, *Wired* declared comment sections an endangered species because so often they become overrun with spam, death threats, racial slurs, and misinformation, and because employing moderators to '[weed] out bad actors' requires running 24–7 operations (Finley, 2016). There remains, however, a strong civil libertarian/free speech ethos with regards to the cybersphere (see Chapter 2), and this was especially dominant during the early years of the internet. Thus, in 2007, Sierra's moderate comment about moderating comments was regarded as an outrageous and unacceptable assault on the liberty of the internet.

The topic Sierra weighed in on did not relate directly to women or to feminism, but the magnitude and misogyny of the abuse she received in response was unmistakably gendered. She received hundreds of rape and death threats, including the 'i hope someone slits your throat and cums down your gob' comment cited in the introduction of this book. Sierra's attackers posted doctored photos which depicted her being choked by undergarments, and with nooses next to her head (Sandoval, 2013). They doxed her by circulating her home address and Social Security number online, alongside false statements about her being a former sex worker and battered wife (Sandoval, 2013). Her antagonists called for the masses to send her material – and the masses obliged. At the time, Sierra commented only briefly on the attack, writing in a final post on her blog: 'I have cancelled all speaking engagements. I am afraid to leave my yard. I will never feel the same. I will never *be* the same' (cited in Walsh, 2007, emphasis in original). After that, she disappeared for years. Not only from the online world but from offline public life as well.

The cyberhate attack on Sierra was one of the first to make international media headlines. Coverage of misogyny online then waned, before resurging in 2011, when a large number of women from many different contexts and countries suddenly – and almost simultaneously – began speaking about the sexualised threats they were receiving via the internet. One of the earliest of this batch of mainstream media reports was published in *The Australian* – the Rupert Murdoch-owned national newspaper I had been working for when I received my first anal rape-mail. In June of 2011, the newspaper published a feature-length piece focusing on high-profile women who had received sexually graphic and threatening 'cyber-bile' (Jackman, 2011). In it, the writer and activist Nina Funnell revealed that her frank, public disclosure about having been indecently assaulted at knife-point had prompted a rash of contributors to websites abusing, attacking, and threatening her. Comments posted about Funnell included: 'what a conceited bitch for thinking she is even worthy of being raped. The guy just probably wanted to give her a good bashing in which case job well done', and 'She's so fugly, I wouldn't even bother raping her from behind with a box cutter' (cited in Jackman, 2011). The same article quoted a contributor to Facebook's Pippa Middleton Arse Appreciation Society page who had boasted that the younger sister of the Duchess of Cambridge 'would need a wheel chair and straw' when he'd finished with her (cited in Jackman, 2011). There was also the following message sent to the activist Julie Gale:

> Shut the fuck up you fucking ugly OLD wowser cunt. You need a good stiff cock shoved down your throat if you ask me. What's the matter? Were you the ugly fat flat chested girl at school? Why don't you shut you fucking cunt mouth? ... you're a ... meddling cunt, who needs to shut the fuck up. I'm going to a brothel tonight, and I'll be selecting the whore who most looks your age. (cited in Jackman, 2011)

Once again, the combination of contempt ('you fucking ugly OLD ... cunt') and lasciviousness ('I'm going to a brothel', etc.) is striking, as is the coercive-sex-as-corrective imagery. Similar themes are apparent in the cyberhate directed at the UK Catholic blogger Caroline Farrow: 'You're gonna scream when you get yours. Fucking slag. Butter wouldn't fucking melt, and you'll cry rape when you get what you've asked for. Bitch' (cited in Thorpe and Rogers, 2011). Farrow, who is married to a vicar, notes that comments about her appearance tend to focus on the fact that she is 'unattractive but yet paradoxically inviting sexual advances' (cited in Lewis, 2011). Like the rest of us sluts, she is also routinely informed that her views on just about everything stem from a deep-seated desire to be anally penetrated alongside a side-serving of being savaged.

These sorts of examples show that the rhetoric of gendered cyberhate has stayed remarkably stable over time, and is almost identical regardless of targets' demographics or location on the socio-political spectrum. In *Damned Whores and God's Police* (1975), the feminist writer Anne Summers argues that the patriarchal cultural tradition in colonial Australia forced women into two rigid stereotypes: damned whores and God's police. A close look at gendered cyberhate suggests these already restrictive social categories are being further compressed in that all women – even those like Farrow who might once have been regarded as God cops – are now being derogated as 'fucking sluts' ('damned whores' being far too polite for modern internet usage).

Accounts of gendered cyberhate continued appearing throughout 2011 in the American, Australian, and British media. In the UK, the journalist Helen Lewis noted the 'sheer volume of sexist abuse thrown at female bloggers' (2011), while the writer Laurie Penny observed that a woman's opinion had become the mini-skirt of the internet in that: 'Having one and flaunting it is somehow asking an amorphous mass of almost-entirely male keyboard-bashers to tell you how they'd like to rape, kill and urinate on you' (2011). These reports prompted a number of women to tell similar stories. Many said they'd assumed they'd been the only ones 'whose every word on the web was greeted with a torrent of abusive, threatening comments' (Lewis, 2012).

Over the course of 2012, mainstream and new media accounts of gendered cyberhate became increasingly routine, and shock at the phenomenon soon made way for resignation. In 2013, one contributor to a popular Australian website began her column with the Austen-esque: 'It's a truth universally acknowledged that a woman in possession of an opinion and a computer will cop a heap of sh*t. Insults, personal attacks and threats of physical violence are par for the course' (Edwards, 2013). In a similarly droll vein, the UK columnist Barbara Ellen noted that being bombarded with public rape threats had become an unavoidable part of female public life, something for an assistant to schedule between meetings: 'Check how many threats my vagina has received today' (2015). While this comment might have been made facetiously, the truth is that some women *were* going to have to begin employing staff to monitor the violent threats being made against their genitals.

Enter the misogynist blitzkrieg that was/is GamerGate.

'I've got a K-bar and I'm coming to your house so I can shove it up your ugly feminist cunt' – #gamergate

The viciousness, vastness, and breadth of GamerGate – the 2014 cyber onslaught against women in gaming (and since then against women in general) – was unprecedented. That said, women in tech and gaming had always been subjected to sustained sexism and an especially noxious version of e-bile. In addition to Sierra's experiences in 2007, there is the aforementioned case of Anita Sarkeesian whose ongoing efforts to draw attention to sexist tropes in video games have rendered her hate-worthy since 2012. Sarkeesian's determination to expose new media misogyny has prompted cyber mob attacks which have included the usual tidal waves of 'rape rape' and 'kill kill' *communiqués,* along with a dash of 'Jew Jew' hate speech for good measure ('So you're a Bolshevik feminist jewess that hates White people... fucking ovendodger' (cited in Mantilla, 2015: 35).)

The 2012 campaign against Sarkeesian resulted in, among much else, her Wikipedia page being vandalised with pornography and altered so that it read she was a 'hooker' who held 'the world record for maximum amount of sexual toys in the posterior' (Greenhouse, 2013), as well as her website and YouTube channel being spammed with abusive comments (Sarkeesian, 2012a, 2012b). The use of 'Google bombing'[5] techniques meant the first result returned by the Google search engine when her name was entered was, 'Anita Sarkeesian is a feminist video blogger and cunt' (Plunkett, 2012). Image-based harassment against Sarkeesian included pornographic photo manipulations (including the ejaculation penis pictures) and 'rape drawings' (including an image of her being sexually assaulted by the Nintendo video game character Mario) (Sarkeesian, 2012b). A 25-year-old Canadian man launched an online game called 'Beat Up Anita Sarkeesian' which invited players to 'punch this bitch in the face' (cited in Sarkeesian, 2012b). With each click on the latter, a photo of Sarkeesian became increasingly bruised and damaged before turning completely red. The experience of women such as Sierra and Sarkeesian is evidence not only of the level of risk faced by women in tech and gaming, but the particular viciousness of at least some members of video gaming cultures.

GamerGate began, prosaically enough, with a bad break-up. The protagonists were a software developer named Eron Gjoni and a feminist indie games designer called Zoë Quinn – a woman who has since earned the dubious title of 'patient zero' of GamerGate (Stuart, 2014b). Gjoni and Quinn met on the online dating site OkCupid and were a couple for five months before breaking up (Jason, 2015). While complaining about ex-partners is obviously not new, the internet enabled the jilted Gjoni to complain about Quinn in a big way to a big audience. He published a blog, nearly 10,000 words long, which he said was a warning to those considering professional or romantic engagement with Quinn (Gjoni cited in Pearl, 2014). *The Zoe Post* claimed that – contrary to Quinn's image as a poster person for equality in gaming – she was actually a selfish, hypocritical, and harmful person, who had cheated on Gjoni with five men (Gjoni 2014; Gjoni cited in Pearl, 2014; Jason, 2015). Gjoni's rant – in which he positions himself as an 'emotional abuse' survivor – is rambling and obsessive, a forensic assemblage of techno dejecta and romantic minutiae in the form of previously private Facebook exchanges, text messages, emails, chat logs, photos, and so on. As one journalist observed, he had weaponised the metadata of his relationship with Quinn into a 'semantic pipe bomb' (Jason, 2015).

Gjoni's personal 'fuck you' was so publicly incendiary because there already existed simmering fury among (mostly) male gamers about the influence of women, feminism, and progressive social values in 'their' boys club. Quinn was already receiving rape and death threats before *The Zoe Post* – mostly because of the popularity of Depression Quest, a quirky game she designed in which players take on the role of a depression sufferer who must juggle mental illness with relationships and jobs (a challenge quite different to, say, the gun- and projectile weapons-based trials of typical first-person shooter games). *The Zoe Post* gave gamers an excuse to rise up against Quinn because in it Gjoni implied his former partner had slept with a journalist to secure positive reviews for her game. Thus GamerGaters had a cover story: the extraordinary attack they were about to launch wasn't about hating on women, it was actually a protest about ethics in video games (known colloquially as 'vidya') journalism. The claim that Quinn had exchanged sex for positive reviews was rapidly exposed as baseless. Even Gjoni (2014) acknowledged that the suggestion was erroneous, saying it had been included in the original version of his blog because of a typographical error. For GamerGaters, however, this inconvenient truth was irrelevant. A brutal new blood sport had begun.

When Gjoni posted his blog on 16 August 2014, it caught the attention of participants associated with 4chan. These people went into what Quinn describes as 'get this bitch' mode, and immediately began circulating her home address and personal photos online (Quinn cited in Stuart, 2014b). Quinn's Wikipedia entry was edited to read: 'Died: soon.' After this entry was deleted, a new one appeared reading: 'Died: October 13, 2014' – the date of her next scheduled public appearance (Jason, 2015). Harassers threatened Quinn's father, and the future employers of her new boyfriend, who subsequently had a pending job offer withdrawn (Jason, 2015). Quinn was inundated with threats such as, 'Im not only a pedophile, ive raped countless teens, this zoe bitch is my next victim, im coming slut', and 'kill yourself. We don't need cunts like you in this world' (Jason, 2015). Incitements to suicide are a common gendered cyberhate tactic, particularly when subjects are known to suffer from mental illness. It was public knowledge, for instance, that Quinn experienced chronic depression (Jason, 2015).

The 'GamerGate' name and hashtag was coined by the Hollywood actor Adam Baldwin who tweeted in support of gamers and linked to videos critical of Quinn. (A year later, Baldwin told a journalist he was surprised but 'very pleased' by the results of his efforts (cited in Bokhari, 2015).) In the midst of all this, Sarkeesian happened to release a new video as part of her ongoing 'Tropes vs Women' series about sexism in gaming (Stuart, 2014b). This re-ignited the conspiracy theory that female scholars were attempting to censor and control games (2014b). Thus what was initially a 'loose affiliation of hardcore gamers' suddenly 'transmogrified into a seething pressure group' (2014b). This transmogrification included an expansion of targets, from Quinn, to supporters of Quinn, to women in the games industry, to female journalists writing about the games industry, to women regarded as 'social justice warriors' (SJW), and then to anyone who made any adverse comments about GamerGate at all: 'The attackers continued to release troves of women's, and some men's, private information and coordinated threats for months. A few even "swatted" their victims, tricking police dispatchers into sending Special Weapons and Tactics (SWAT) teams to raid women's homes' (Jason, 2015).

Quinn fled her home shortly after the assault began (Stuart, 2014b). After having received such a massive quantity of abuse, her concern was that it would only be a matter of time before one of her anonymous critics eventually made good on their threats to kill her (Quinn cited in Stuart, 2014b). In the same month – August, 2014 – Sarkeesian also left her home after receiving a series of graphic death threats which demonstrated knowledge of her and her parents' home addresses (Marcetic, 2014). Shortly after this, Sarkeesian cancelled a speaking event at Utah State University after an anonymous emailer threatened 'the deadliest school shooting in American history' if her talk went ahead as planned (cited in Marcetic, 2014). This email said Sarkeesian was 'everything wrong with the feminist woman' and would 'die screaming like the craven little whore that she is' (Marcetic, 2014). Around the same time, the personal details of the American games designer Brianna Wu – the co-founder of the Boston game studio Giant Spacekat – were posted on the 8chan web site, and within minutes someone tweeted at her saying,

'I've got a K-bar[6] and I'm coming to your house so I can shove it up your ugly feminist cunt' (cited in Stuart, 2014a). Wu also left her home because she feared for her safety. Her observation was that this was 'not just casual sexism', it was 'angry, violent sexism ... Every woman I know in the industry is scared. Many have thought about quitting' (cited in Stuart, 2014a).

GamerGaters and their fans and apologists remain extremely vocal and occasionally organised. In the aftermath of the initial attacks, they have also driven fierce debate about whether journalistic and academic coverage of GamerGate has been fair. Some point to a 2015 Women, Action, and the Media (WAM!) report about harassment on Twitter (Matias et al., 2015), which they say proves that less than 1 per cent of GamerGate-supporting Twitter accounts are harassing accounts, and that the dominant mainstream media narrative about GamerGate is therefore a 'lie' (Wohling, 2015; see also Rahman, 2015). The 'less than 1 per cent' reading, however, does not hold water because the study was simply not designed to investigate the percentage of GamerGaters sending harassment. Noting the clamour for clarification on this point, the lead author of the WAM! report said he was hesitant to comment after GamerGater supporters 'flooded' his Twitter feed during his PhD qualifying exams (Matias, 2015). He did, however, reiterate that 'very little' could be learned about GamerGate from the study because the researchers did not have the data to 'make any representative claims, positive or negative, about any specific subgroup online, including GamerGate' (Matias, 2015).

Another study frequently cited by GamerGaters reports that use of misogynist language on social media could be an equal opportunity phenomenon. In 2016, the Demos think tank published the results of an analysis focusing on the use of the words 'slut' and 'whore' on Twitter, and suggesting that half of aggressively misogynistic tweets are sent by women (see: 'The use of misogynistic terms on Twitter', 2016; Dale, 2016). This followed a 2014 Demos report suggesting that women are just as comfortable using misogynistic language as men (Bartlett et al., 2014). The opaque methodologies of the 2016 study, however, have been roundly debunked by the forensic corpus linguist Claire Hardaker (2016; see also Criado-Perez, 2016). Among multiple methodological issues, Hardaker critiques the use of an ill-explained 'natural language processing algorithm' which supposedly allows Demos' computers to recognise meaning in language in the same way humans would. Pointing out the manifest failures of software supposed to convince people they are talking to other people, Hardaker observes that computers make 'colossal screw ups' when confronted with messy features of language such as 'sarcasm, threats, allusions, in-jokes, novel metaphors, clever wordplay, typographical errors, slang, mock impoliteness, and so on' (2016). Anyone familiar with the basic tenets of reception studies would also be highly suspicious of claims that a computer could divine the single, 'true' meaning of a given media text or personal communication. (In fact, a computer able to respond to meaning in language like a human would need to be capable of arguing boisterously with other computers about whose interpretation is the most defensible, possibly over a beer or a glass of cheeky white.)

In late 2015, meanwhile, the writer Cathy Young[7] mused – in a piece largely sympathetic to the GamerGate campaign – that, apart from the ISIS/Daesh Islamic extremists, it was hard to think of a contemporary movement with a worse image (Young, 2015b). Young suggests that the harassment of Quinn, Sarkeesian, and Wu may have come from 'third-party trolls' and that the 'misogynist hate group' line being run by anti-GamerGaters is erasing and silencing the voices of women who support or are active members of the GamerGate movement (Young, 2015b). More generally, pro-GamerGaters claim that the campaign has been misunderstood, inaccurately represented, and used as a scapegoat, and that critics of the movement are hypocrites because GamerGaters and their supporters have also been doxed, threatened with violence, and abused (for an example of the latter, see the 'slackjawed pickletits' comments from the former NFL player Chris Kluwe (2014) in Chapter 3). Some GamerGaters go so far as to allege that women are fabricating abuse and death threats as part of elaborate 'false flag' operations including faked screen shots calculated to wrongly impugn gamers (Robertson, 2014).

While it is true that some GamerGaters are women and that some GamerGaters have been attacked online by anti-GamerGaters, this does not mean the movement is not misogynist. Diehard GamerGaters insist that the campaign has only ever been about ethics in games journalism, yet the group's targets continue to be almost exclusively female games developers, academics, and writers, and its undercurrents have always been 'darkly misogynistic' (Stuart, 2014b). The argument that various incidents of misogynist harassment conducted in the GamerGate name are not the work of 'true' GamerGaters is also unconvincing. After going to great lengths to investigate these so-called 'real' GamerGaters, the journalist Jesse Singal urged participants to come clean about their anti-progressivism political motivations:

> With you guys, any bad thing that happens is, by definition, not the work of A True Gamergater. It's one of the oldest logical fallacies in the book ... Say what you will about the tenets of anti-progressivism, dude ... at least it's an ethos ... (2014)

Following Singal, my view is that a key GamerGate motivation is indeed resentment at the incursion of women – with all their perceived SJW values, aesthetics, and politics – into what is regarded as male turf.

As with the attacks on Sierra, GamerGate marked another critical moment in the evolution of gendered cyberhate: a moment where the circulation of misogynist cyberhate was no longer the exception but the rule. We could call it the moment the internet reached peak Rapeglish, except that, as yet, there is no sign the deluge is easing. Sierra, meanwhile, has decided she actually got off easy when she was first attacked so viciously:

> Most of the master trolls weren't active on Twitter in 2007. Today, they, along with their friends, fans, followers, and a zoo of anonymous sock puppet accounts[8] are. The time from troll-has-an-idea to troll-mobilizes-brutal-assault has shrunk from weeks to minutes. Twitter, for all its good, is a hate amplifier. (Sierra, 2014)

To illustrate the amplification of various aspects of gendered cyberhate at a more general level, I offer the following addendum to the previous textbox. As with the latter, this is not a rigid matrix, but is designed to offer a rough guide to some of the ways gendered cyberhate has altered since around 2010.

CHANGES IN GENDERED CYBERHATE SINCE CIRCA 2010

- Vast expansion of the number of attackers and targets.
- Vast expansion of the number and types of channels used for attack (for example, cyberhate may involve: messages sent to private email addresses; posts on public boards and in those below-the-line comment sections that still exist; direct tweeting; blogs; Facebook pages dedicated to attacks; dating apps; online gaming, and so on).

- Vast expansion of attack modes (for example, predominantly text-based attacks are increasingly likely to be augmented by image-based harassment (especially the sending of unsolicited 'dick pics'), as well as approaches such as Wikipedia vandalism, Google bombing, revenge porn, 'sextortion', identity theft, impersonation, rape blackmail videos, cyberstalking, and so on).
- Vast expansion in the types of women targeted (alongside an increase in attacks explicitly framed as responses to feminist activism and/or perceived feminist gains).
- Increased likelihood of attacks initiated by groups such as those related to video game communities, GamerGate, and men's rights organisations.
- Increased mob activity (as well as much *larger* mob activity).
- Planned and coordinated attacks as part of group strategies.
- Dramatic increases in the longevity of attacks (some continuing for years or having ongoing status).
- Increases in the identifiability of attackers (anonymity online becoming increasingly difficult due to, for example, Facebook's 'real name' policies).
- Obsessive, *en masse* focus on particular women (for example, on Sarkeesian and Quinn).
- Marked amplification of abuse in the aftermath of abuse being exposed or spoken about publicly.
- Increases in the reported suffering of and impact on targets.
- Increases in the frequency, severity, specificity, and credibility of threats such that targets are more likely to give them credence and take offline action (such as cancelling public engagements and leaving their homes).
- Increases in the number and types of attacks which begin online but then move (or at least are designed to appear as if they are about to move) offline in the form of doxing, swatting, bomb and death threats, inciting others to attack targets offline, contacting targets' employers, demonstrating knowledge of targets' home addresses by organising items to be delivered, and so on.

'the exact same guy' – e-bile algebra

This chapter has drawn attention to some of the changes that have occurred in gendered cyberhate over time. It has also identified a significant constant:

namely, that the rhetoric of Rapeglish is extraordinarily similar despite the year it is sent, the channel via which it travels, and the woman it targets. In this way, gendered e-bile has a quasi-algebraic quality in that the names of the senders and receivers can be substituted endlessly without altering the structure of the discourse. It is reminiscent of the material produced by online generators: computer programs such as the postmodern essay generator, the porn star name generator, and the Shakespearean insult generator which cut and paste textual fragments to produce humorously-themed randomness based on a range of pre-determined parameters. (Interestingly, it was an automated wordfilter on 4chan's /b/ board that, in 2008, began changing 'femanon' – a pejorative portmanteau for a female member of a male-dominated online community – to 'cumdumpster' – thus popularising the latter term; (Manivannan, 2013).) While this book does not possess the requisite ones and zeroes to host its own Rapeglish generator, I can offer the following potential input data drawn from real-life examples (complete with real-life whimsical spellings). To operate, simply take any entry from beneath each of the columns marked A to H and place these together to generate your very own representative – if not particularly singular – example of Rapeglish.

RAPEGLISH GENERATOR

While I continued to add material to the Rapeglish generator throughout the writing of this book, I quickly reached a saturation point vis-à-vis themes. For example, the vast bulk of the adjectives used to describe women relate to unattractiveness, mental incapacity, and/or problematic sexuality. After that, antagonists seem to run out of ideas (although threatening to 'ducktape' a woman before she is 'berried' alive could indicate a degree of imaginative ability). I note, too, that the above does not indicate the frequency of certain rhetorical constructs. For example, cyberhate in the form of hostile wishful thinking such as, 'I hope you get raped with a chainsaw' (cited in Doyle, 2011a), is extremely common. There is evidence to suggest perpetrators are aware that such sentence constructions might offer legal loopholes. For example, in Australia in 2016, police issued a warning to a Twitter user who had been sending direct death threats to the Australian media personality Waleed Aly and his wife – referred to as a 'hijabi scumfuk floozie' (cited in A. Lattouf, personal communication, 27 May 2016). Of his dealings with law enforcement, this man said the police had been 'pretty

A salutation	B adjective	C noun	D punctuation (optional)	E transitional phrase	F outcome part one	G outcome part two	H rationale
Fuck you, you	unrapeable	cunt	.	I hope you	die of pussy cancer	while your children watch	coz you're a stupid feminist asshole.
Eat my cock, you	worthless	bitch	,	soon you will	take a bath with a toaster	as I spit on your arse	coz you're asking for it.
Kill yourself, you	delusional	e-skank	;	we will ensure you	deepthroat a chainsaw	so we can cum in what's left of your cock-stuffed gash	coz you don't know shit.
Your mother sucks cock in hell, you	ugly	attention whore	...	it's just a matter of time til you	go to jail and get ass fucked by a demon	until you rot	coz you're an ugly fucking cunt.
I'd never bang you, you	obese	dyke	–	Ima make sure you	choke on my cock	while I shoot a hot load into the wound	coz you're a screeching bitch.
Hello, you	slutty	piece of shit	:	what you deserve is to	have your arse split by my cock	while your vagina isn't being used for shit	coz #ihopeyougetraped.
Listen up, you	hysterical	scrubmuffin	etc	me and my friends will laugh while you	take a thick rope and put it round your neck	on account of your epic unfuck-ability	coz you're a cum-guzzling lesbo.

(Continued)

(Continued)

A salutation	B adjective	C noun	D punctuation (optional)	E transitional phrase	F outcome part one	G outcome part two	H rationale
Fucking shut it, you	unfuckable	heifer		the internet will watch while you	taste your shit off my dick	to put an end to your blithering bullshit	coz of your whore face.
Hey, you	bitter	hole		get back in the kitchen and	drink bleach	while anal sex wipes the smirk off your face	coz you need an attitude adjustment.
You need dick, you	misandrist	hag		9000 penises will facefuck you while you	get raped to death with a gorsebrush	then I'll gang bang your slut daughter	coz you're a stupid little girl.
Wassup, you	castrating	retard		make me a sammich as you	have your head removed	while a bullet rips through your brainstem	coz you're trash talking fuckmeat.
Stop breathing, you	humourless	slut		I'm gonna pistol whip you over and over until you	jump off a bridge	and I finish off in your eyes	coz you're an intellectual lightweight.
Everyone will jump on the rape train, you	stupid	tranny		first we will mutilate your genitals with scissors while you	find the corpse of your cat	so I can stick an egg in your vagina and punch it	coz you look like you got Downs.

A salutation	B adjective	C noun	D punctuation (optional)	E transitional phrase	F outcome part one	G outcome part two	H rationale
Open that cunt wide bitch, you	whining	feminazi		check out this hot pic of my gauntlet as you	are used for your one and only purpose in this world	and have the crazy fucked out of you	coz you're a faggot embracing douche fag.
I have a sniper rifle aimed directly at your head, you	old	man-looking whore		fuck your father til you	lose consciousness	and beg to die at 8pm tonight	coz I've just got out of prison and would happily do more time to see you berried!! #tenfeetunder
Kiss your pussy goodbye, you	white/ black/ Asian	carpet-munching witch		get down on your knees while you	watch me rip your neck open	and fuck the gaping hole	coz you should have been aborted with a hanger.
UR DEAD AND GONE TONIGHT, YOU	lying	SJW cunt		beg for mercy while you	get dry raped	and smashed up the fuckhole	coz silence is golden but ducktape is silver.
Watch out, you	man-hating	feminist		now you will	gag on my rod	til you learn to shut your damn mouth	coz you're an unrapeable slut.

cool' and had told him: 'you know where the line is, [you're] right up against it and if you step over it again you'll be leaving here in cuffs." That was pretty much it' (A. Lattouf, 2016). In an interview with the journalist Antoinette Lattouf, this man said the police warning had not persuaded him to back down, and that he would ramp up his efforts online:

> It's now just informed me of where the line is. Don't make explicit threats but it's not so bad to make a veiled threat. So absolutely I will say stuff again, I will just word it more carefully. I'll still challenge and ridicule and mock. (cited in A. Lattouf, 2016)

He then unleashed what Lattouf describes as a torrent of abusive threats, including: 'I hope #WaleedAly ACCIDENTLY cuts his throat while shaving' (A. Lattouf, 2016, emphasis in original).

The tedious predictability of misogynist discourse online is not lost on targets, who sometimes cite it as a source of amusement. The website Fat, Ugly or Slutty, for instance, provides a taxonomy of remarks received by female gamers, filing comments in categories such as 'Crudely Creative', 'Unprovoked Rage', 'Lewd Proposals', 'Death Threats', 'Repeat Offender', and 'Sandwich Making 101' ('You play video games? So are you fat, ugly or slutty?', n.d.). (The last item on the list refers to the internet catchphrase 'make me a sandwich' – often deliberately misspelled as 'make me a sammich'. It references the idea that women belong in the kitchen.)

Sady Doyle, meanwhile, provides a revealing summary of the material re-tweeted via the #MenCallMeThings hashtag on Twitter. She identifies a number of themes, including: the claim that female targets are weak, over-sensitive, hysterical, and irrational; the suggestion that female targets are both whores and yet 'not worth fucking'; and assorted threats of violence (2011b). She also notes the 'overwhelmingly impersonal, repetitive, stereo-typed quality' of the abuse, as well as the fact that 'all of us are being called the same things, in the same tone':

> What matters is not which guys said it: What matters is that, when you put their statements side-by-side, they all sound like *the exact same guy*. And when you look at what they're saying ... they always sound like they're speaking to *the exact same woman*. When men are using the same insults and sentiments to shut down women ... we know that it's not about us; it's about gender. (Doyle, 2011b, emphasis in original)

Doyle is spot on. Many women are being abused online *because* they are women, reflecting a tenacious – and possibly worsening – sexism in the broader community. These new articulations of old misogyny rely on hyperbolic and sexualised derision that is both intensely intimate and entirely impersonal, in that the hate directed at one woman is all but indistinguishable from that directed at another. It is a perverse – and revealing – paradox that the most personal of insults, attacks and threats can seem generic, routine, and banal as a result of their pervasiveness. The ubiquity of Rapeglish in the contemporary cybersphere is both a result of as well as constitutive of the normalisation of this discourse. We should not, however, accept the common advice that rape and death threats be shrugged off as a trivial internet annoyance on par with pop-up ads or scam emails. As I will go on to explain, gendered cyberhate targets can experience profound suffering, and this suffering is exacerbated by institutional neglect and advice such as 'just laugh it off'.

While feminism is certainly a lightning rod for male antagonists, it is also important to note that girls and women are being attacked not just for turning up online to do feminism or politics, but for turning up online *to do anything at all*. Karen Cohen, a former YouTube executive, has confessed to being routinely shocked by the hate directed at female users posting even the most quotidian content: 'here were these creators putting up DIY fishtail braid videos, and there were people telling them, "I want to rape you" in the comment section' (cited in Moran, 2015). The actor Ashley Judd (2015), meanwhile, received what she describes as a 'tsunami' of rape threats, gender-based violence, and misogyny simply for tweeting a comment about a basketball game. Women are being abused and threatened with sexual violence for commenting on bike-riding, comic book covers, and soft pretzel recipes (Mantilla, 2015: 29, 30 37). This provides further support for my argument that to properly understand the contemporary epidemic of gendered cyberhate, we must change gears by shifting the focus *away* from the contexts, politics, and actions of the women under attack and *towards* the men doing the attacking.

Notes

1 For further discussion of this see Jane, 2014b, 2014c, 2014d.
2 My understanding of 'Wood' in this context is that it is a colloquial reference to an erect penis.
3 The slang term 'owned' is defined by an *Urban Dictionary* contributor as being 'physically or mentally disgraced' in a formidable manner (dude, 2008).
4 Online identities need not correlate with a computer user's offline identity in order to be recognisable. For instance, it is common for created personas to become well-known in cyber communities.

5   'Google bombing' is a term used to describe the manipulation of the Google
     search engine so that web users searching for a specific term are directed to
     content determined by the bombers.
6   My reading of 'K-bar' here is that it is a misspelling of 'ka-bar' – a combat knife.
7   With regard to Young's standpoint on GamerGate, I note that she has her own
     political agenda, including a rejection of contemporary versions of social justice
     as a 'cultish' and 'totalitarian' ideology (Young, 2015a). Indeed, Young's views
     have resulted in other feminists labelling her a 'professional female misogynist'
     and 'rape apologist' (Marcotte, 2014).
8   'Sock puppets' are fake accounts used for various purposes, including the imper-
     sonation of targets.

2

WHY IT IS SO

Because they can

This chapter looks at the 'whys' of gendered cyberhate. It is the shortest chapter in this book for a reason. By my account, the etiology of gendered cyberhate is relatively simple. Further, as I will go on to show in Chapter 4, making it more complex than necessary risks contributing to the broader exculpation of perpetrators.

So, why are so many men calling so many women ugly, fat, and slutty on the internet?

1. Because men continue to hold a disproportionate share of the political, economic, and social power, some using various forms of violence to keep women in their place; and
2. Because – thanks to the design and dominant norms of the contemporary cybersphere – they can.

With regard to point one, there is a wealth of evidence showing that the world remains deeply divided along gendered lines. Women make up only 17 per cent of government ministers globally, earn on average only 60 to 75 per cent of men's wages, and carry most of the caring responsibility for children, the elderly, and the sick, spending as much as 10 times more unpaid care work than men (Smith, 2016). More than a third of women suffer physical and/or sexual violence over the course of their lives (Smith, 2016). Feminist attempts to address these inequities often meet with a vicious backlash. In April 2016, for instance, an Australian university group announced it would stage an awareness-raising cup-cake stall selling baked goods priced to reflect various pay gaps. A white man would be charged $1 per cup-cake, while a woman of colour in the legal profession would pay only 55c. Threats of rape, violence, and death rained down in the cyber-sphere. 'Anonymous keyboard warriors' directed their contempt and fury not only against the bake sale organisers but against all those 'ugly chicks', 'fucking scum', and 'feminist cunts' likely to attend (cited in Price, 2016).

The second point, above, refers to those aspects of the cybersphere which make it so very easy for people to abuse and harass each other with impunity. The advent of the web 2.0 era,[1] the spectacular uptake of social media, and the historical ability to use the internet with relative anonymity has created networked environments that lend themselves to drive-by attacks as well as the galvanisation of aggressive mobs. These features of the cybersphere, however, are *general* features. While they explain the mechanisms that allow people to speak in such a disinhibited fashion (the medium), they are connected to but do not fully explain the content of this speech (the message). This is why the first point of the two-part answer above is as critical as the second. That so many men are using the Ring of Gyges[2] opportunities offered by the internet to abuse so many women is both diagnostic and constitutive of the systemic gender inequities discussed above. As the columnist Katha Pollitt puts it, new technology has allowed 'this cadre of incredibly enraged men' to all find each other (cited in Goldberg, 2015). To a certain extent it also means that discourse in the cybersphere can be used as a litmus test of the sorts of community attitudes that exist below the surface but that are no longer considered acceptable to express in 'polite' company.

It is tempting to conclude this chapter here – at just over a page. As I will go on to show, attempts to offer more complex explanations about the reasons for gendered cyberhate often have the effect of letting men off the hook. Narrowly focusing on the particularities of individual incidents tends to elide the broader misogyny problem, while the insistence that perpetrators' motivations be unearthed and given due consideration often leads to – or indeed *proceeds from* – the conclusion/'conclusion' that such discourse is little more than misunderstood humour on par with blokey pub banter.

This book, however, promises a history of misogyny online and, to this end, I will extend the 'why is it so?' inquiry further. This will help show how and why a domain whose founders had such idealistic hopes for participatory equality has become such a bastion of abusive exclusion. It explains the way the naïve egalitarianism of the early cyber-pioneers (who rejected identity-markers such as gender), the aspirations for the internet to be a place that did not require regulators (because it was about self-governance, after all), and the relative anonymity of the net has together fostered the development of a culture that not only permits but *rewards* misogyny, a place where Rapeglish has become the norm.

As such, the remainder of this chapter will examine, from a Michel Foucault-inspired perspective, those aspects of the history of the internet which constitute some of the conditions of possibility for the prevalence (as well as the form and content) of contemporary misogyny online, as well as the continuing *laissez-faire* approach to regulatory interventions. The latter is especially relevant to Chapter 5, in that it helps explain why people in various positions of power, authority, and influence are regarded as making some sense when they respond to gendered cyberhate with comments such as, 'trolls are just misunderstood pranksters', 'women should just leave the internet', and (a personal favourite for reasons I will explain presently) 'toughen up, princess'.

'Our world is different … it is not where bodies live'

Many of the pioneers of the early internet were anti-capitalist idealists (Barker and Jane, 2016: 181). Tim Berners-Lee, the English engineer and computer scientist credited with 'inventing' the internet in 1989, could have made a fortune if he'd exploited his idea for global networked computers as a money-making enterprise. Instead, he persuaded his employers that it should be offered to the world as a free resource (Naughton, 2014). Consider, too, the views of the US writer and cyberlibertarian John Perry Barlow, who, in 1996, published 'A Declaration of the Independence of Cyberspace' in which he declared that the governments of the industrial world should keep their distance from this emerging global social space. Barlow's grand challenge to the powers-that-be in what was then known colloquially as the 'meat' world was that:

> You have no sovereignty where we gather … You have no moral right to rule us nor do you possess any methods of enforcement we have true reason to fear … You do not know our culture, our ethics, or the unwritten codes that already provide our society more order than could be obtained by any of your impositions.

> You claim there are problems among us that you need to solve ... Many of these problems don't exist. Where there are real conflicts, where there are wrongs, we will identify them and address them by our means ... Our world is different ... it is not where bodies live. (Barlow, 1996)

Decades later, the idea that 'the web and money just weren't seen as things that went together' (Aleks Krotoski cited in Crossley-Holland, 2010) is laughably quaint. Barlow's manifesto, meanwhile, seems, at best, naïve; at worst, a dangerous conceit. On some points, he was right. Industrial world governments – those 'weary giants of flesh and steel' (Barlow, 1996) – have indeed struggled to find fit-for-purpose enforcement methods with which to respond to online crime. Moreover, plenty of online communities *do* operate by unwritten codes that are mysterious and opaque to outsiders. But Barlow's belief that the cybersphere would be a world where 'all may enter without privilege or prejudice accorded by race, economic power, military force, or station of birth' (1996) would prove to be dead wrong.

Traditional constraints such as class, race, culture, gender, sex, and sexuality have all emerged as key markers of difference and inequality in terms of access to technology and engagement online (see Flew, 2004; Nakamura and Chow-White, 2012; Van Deursen and Van Dijk, 2014). Barlow (1996) was also mistaken in his insistence that the cybersphere was mostly problem-free and that any 'real' conflict or wrongs would be identified and addressed in-house by digital natives. This is partly because of disagreement about what phenomena constitute problems – and therefore what interventions constitute solutions. For members of key subcultural trolling communities, for instance, the *real* gender problem online is that gender is ever mentioned on the internet at all. From their perspective, the correct response should include the ritual humiliation, punishment, and ostracisation of any female online who refers to the fact that she is female.

'Equil!'

The etymology of 'GTFO' provides a useful entry point for understanding the rationale of those internet dwellers who simultaneously insist: (a) that gender is irrelevant online because cyberspace is an egalitarian space; and (b) that any woman who reveals her gender should pay. The full version of the catchphrase is actually 'Tits or GTFO', which originated on 4chan as a response to posters identifying as female (Marwick, 2014: 66). At first blush, the imperative seems easy enough to understand: 'show us your breasts or leave'. Yet, in many cases, the message functions more along the lines of, 'show us your breasts, then leave while we abuse you for agreeing to show us your breasts'.

Internet insider explanations about what 'Tits or GTFO' means vary and are often contradictory. In a YouTube video entitled '4chan explains the true meaning of "Tits or GTFO!"', a 4chan regular who goes by the name of Mundane Matt insists the expression does not mean women are only welcome in an online space if they show their breasts (2014). Matt goes to great lengths to explain that the use of 'Tits or GTFO' is actually about preserving the early ideal of gender-free anonymity online – that is, it is about ensuring the cyberspace is a level playing field rather than about the exclusion of women. The coherence of his explanation falters, however, when he acknowledges that the supposedly erroneous reading of 'Tits or GTFO' also has some truth because, in fact, 'everyone likes tits ... it's like kind of a thing' (2014).

Thus we can see that many men on the internet do want to see – and indeed often pressure women to perform or display – overt and normative feminine sexuality. At the same time, however, they punish women for acquiescing to these demands, all the while claiming to occupy an internet moral high ground. The 'logic' goes something along the lines of: *Women must be sexual for men. Men must punish women for being sexual (and also – paradoxically – for not being sexual). Men must not be punished for punishing women for these things because they are operating in the internet's best interests.* It is a perfect example of the contempt/desire/disavowal dynamic discussed in Chapter 1.

The rhetoric of GTFO-related contributions on Reddit and 4chan provides further support for this reading. Here is a post from one of the 'anons' on 4chan's /b/ 'random' board:

People (Women mostly) Seem to forget why we have Tits or GTFO. Because we would get these shameless attention whores coming here, demanding our attention because they have a vagina. We are all anon, No face No gender Nothing to set up apart from one another. Equil! ... Your being female HAS NO FUCKING RELEVANCE! We don't care what your fucking gender is! We are Not asking for it so don't broadcast it! To fight this we invented Tits or GTFO. This was done as a deterrent to shun away the attention whores. If you do show Tits and Vag with time stamp, your just in the end confirming what we all thank about you. You are an attention WHORE, your Whoring your body out for attention. You shame yourself by doing this. You only have yourself to blame. Because GET THE FUCK OUT is always a choice. (Anonymous cited in Black Poison Soul, 2014)

Another contributor adds:

one of the rules of the internet is 'there are no girls on the internet'. This rule does not mean what you think it means. In real life, people like you for being a girl. They want to fuck you, so they pay attention to you and they pretend what you have to say is interesting, or that you are smart or clever. On the internet, we don't have the chance to fuck you. This means the advantage of being a 'girl' does not exist. You don't get a bonus to conversation just because I'd like to put my cock in you... [but] ...you want your girl-advantage back, because you are too vapid and too stupid to do or say anything interesting without it. You are forgetting the rules, there are no girls on the internet. The one exception to this rule, the one way you can get your 'girlness' back on the internet, is to post your tits. This is, and should be, degrading for you, an admission that the only interesting thing about you is your naked body. tl;dr[3]: tits or GET THE FUCK OUT. (StilRH, 2014)

Comments such as the above show that the supposedly identity-free anonymity and 'equility' advocated and celebrated online is now strongly linked to a toxic, *ressentiment*-fuelled masculinity. Note, too, the way the language and examples offered contradict the putative propositional content of the posts. By insisting so strenuously that gender is irrelevant online – but by prosecuting this case via the rhetoric of slut shaming as well as by framing women's value as being first and foremost about their function as sex objects – comments such as the above demonstrate that these internet communities are *absolutely* gendered and *extremely* hostile to women.

Moreover, the claim that everyone is treated with equal irreverence online simply doesn't wash given that much of the sexist, racist, homophobic, ableist, and transphobic discourse generated on sites such as Reddit and 4chan is – as far as researchers can tell – often the work of young, relatively affluent white men. In her ethnographies of subcultural trolling communities, Whitney Phillips, notes that trolling is explicitly androcentric and an 'absolute sausagefest'[4] in terms of participant demographics (2015a: 82). Adrian Chen, meanwhile, observes that the trolls he has researched are predominantly younger white men from middle America (cited in Lewis, 2013). These observations comport with experience of cyberhate targets such as Jess Phillips, who says most of her thousands of attackers are based in the US (cited in Oppenheim, 2016).

Viral misogyny

In the previous section, I showed the way the identity-free 'all may enter without privilege or prejudice' ideals associated with the pioneers of cyberspace have mutated into subcultural norms which facilitate, enforce, and rationalise aggressive androcentrism and toxic misogyny. A key element of this transition has involved the mainstream uptake of the sexist vitriol that circulated in the name of humour during the 'golden age' of subcultural trolling from 2008 to 2011 (Phillips, 2015b). The /b/ board of the imageboard site 4chan has long been known for its cute cat photos as well as its violent fetish pornography, its child pornography, its racist and sexist rants, its gory photos, and its anarchic, anonymous atmosphere – one reminiscent of the earliest days of the web (Stryker, 2011: 13–14).

Equally infamous are the 'subreddit' sections of the social news site Reddit. The latter was the haunt of Violentacrez, a man at one time known as 'the biggest troll on the web' (Chen, 2012a). Violentacrez created and/ or moderated subreddits such as 'Jailbait', 'Chokeabitch', 'Niggerjailbait', 'Rapebait', 'Jewmerica', 'Incest', and 'Creepshots' (Chen, 2012a). Creepshots featured sexualised photos taken covertly of women in public, usually close-ups of their breasts or buttocks. Jailbait, meanwhile, involved users posting snapshots of scantily-clad tween and teenage girls. Violentacrez's trolling career was derailed in 2012 when the *Gawker* journalist Adrian Chen outed him as Michael Brutsch, a 49-year-old military father and financial services company programmer who was fired within a day of Chen's *exposé* being published (Chen, 2012a, 2012b). At the height of his reign as Violentacrez, however, Brutsch was named the most important 'Redditor' of 2011 by *The Daily Dot* (Morris, 2011). He was, to use Chen's words, 'the most influential user of one of the most influential websites on the internet' (2012a).

The Violentacrez/Brutsch case study illustrates the power and influence of trolls and their particular online habitats. While it is true that venues such as 4chan and Reddit have spawned distinct internet subcultures, they are not niche sites. Five years after 4chan was launched in 2003, it was receiving more than 200 million page views per month (Schwartz, 2008). In 2010, its founder boasted that, after starting out with only 20 users, 4chan had become the largest active forum in the US, with 8.2 million unique visitors every month and 600 million page loads per month (Moot cited in Bilton, 2010). Reddit's vital statistics are even more impressive. Over the course of 2015, it attracted 82.54 billion page views, 73.15 million submissions, and 725.85 million comments made by 8.7 million authors (Unknown, 2015). Its legitimacy hit a high in 2012 when President Barack Obama participated in a question and answer session on the site (Chen, 2012a).

The size and sway of venues such as 4chan and Reddit shows that while internet trolls may have had subcultural and transgressive origins, in the contemporary cybersphere, trolling activities, trollish humour, and the trolling ethos have become the – immensely powerful – status quo. As E. Gabriella Coleman observes, trolls have transformed 'occasional and sporadic acts' of flaming into 'a full-blown set of cultural norms and set of linguistic practices' (2012: 110). My observation is that these have been enthusiastically taken up by the mainstream internet community. Compassion, immanent reflection, earnestness of any kind – these things are anathema to the trolling ethos which demands that 'nothing is sacred or off limits' (Landers, n.d.). Media critiques are sneeringly appropriated to become yet more grist for the meme[5] machine. Humiliating and sometimes privacy-invading revenge is enacted on critics. And the joke is usually at the expense of someone else – often a someone else who is female, queer, or of colour.

Early subcultural trolls should therefore be seen as such powerful figures not just because there are so many of them or because their sites have become so popular, but because their cultures, *modi operandi*, and speaking styles have become such a dominant (arguably *the* dominant) tenor of so much internet discourse. This is especially true with respect to graphic and hyperbolic misogyny which has migrated from troll sites into the mainstream, in much the same way that 'image macros'[6] have become viral phenomena. The influence of troll subcultures is also apparent in those aspects of misogynist cyberhate which involve perfor-mance, game play, and competition among antagonists. Similarly, mob attacks on women are reminiscent of 4chan-style trolling raids (that is, coordinated attacks on sites or individuals).

The norms and practices of subcultural trolling communities provide important background context for the gendered cyberhate story. But they do not fully account for the reasons the masses have taken to troll-style rape jokes and sexualised vitriol with such enthusiasm. Structural misogyny, in contrast, *does* explain why so many Joe Internets surveyed 4chan and Reddit's offerings and decided to pick up and run with the hyperbolic and violent sexism. Clearly many men found this discourse both intelligible and appealing. Part of the attraction likely relates to a backlash against 'political correctness' in that people are carving out online environments 'purely to express the type of racist, homophobic, or sexist speech that is no longer acceptable in public society, at work, or even at home' (Marwick cited in Lewis, 2013). For Karla Mantilla, it also exemplifies the 'massive cultural defense mechanism[s]' – that is, the backlashes – which have emerged in response to previous feminist mobilisations against other forms of misogynistic attacks such as domestic violence, rape and date rape, stalking, street harassment, and sexual harassment in the workplace (2015: 17, 159).

As such, the contemporary proliferation of gendered cyberhate is best understood as emerging from a combination of new technologies, subcultural capital and appropriation, individual psychologies, mob dynamics, and, most importantly, systemic gender inequity (including a backlash against feminist gains and activism). Misogynists have never had so many opportunities to collectivise and abuse women with so few consequences. Female targets have never been so visible and instantly accessible in such large numbers. The increasing personalisation of the internet also means that, more and more often, Facebook and Google are tailoring material to match users' preferences. Thus sexist modes of engagement are continually reinforced and it has become increasingly easy to inhabit a 'filter bubble'[7] where 'cum dumpster' is the accepted synonym for 'female' and the standard response to any woman who complains is to call her an unfuckable cunt, before bombarding her with unsolicited photos of one's penis.

If this doesn't sound particularly equil, the anons of 4 chan will no doubt be happy to remind you that GETTING THE FUCK OUT is always a choice. As I will show in the next chapter, however, in this context the most apt expression is not 'choice' but 'coercion'.

Notes

1   The term 'web 2.0' – in contrast with 'web 1.0' – refers to changes in the web which facilitate user-generated content, interactivity, collaboration, and sharing.
2   The Ring of Gyges – from Plato's *Republic* – granted its wearers invisibility, and often features in ethics-related thought experiments about how individuals might act if they are able to do so without fear of being caught and punished.

3   'tl;dr' is a contraction used online for 'too long; don't read'.
4   'Sausagefest' is a slang term referring to the presence of a large number of men.
5   Coleman defines 'memes' as 'viral images, videos, and catchphrases under con-
     stant modification by users, and with a propensity to travel as fast as the Internet
     can move them' (2012: 109).
6   'Image macro' is a catch-all term for photos overlaid with humorous or ironic
     text.
7   'Filter bubble' is Eli Pariser's term (2011) to describe the way the personalisation
     strategies adopted by corporations such as Google and Facebook are changing
     our experiences of the internet in that algorithms are curating the content based
     on users' previous online activity.

3

HITTING HOME

'Hi fat bitch. I see this is where you live'

Kath Read[1] writes with humour, profanity, and what she (quite accurately) describes as 'a really solid "fuck you" vibe'. The Australian librarian in her early 40s is a feminist whose activism focuses on the politics of being fat in a society that worships thin. Since around 2009, she has used social media platforms such as Twitter, Facebook, and Tumblr, as well as a WordPress blog called 'Fat Heffalump: Living with Fattitude', to push back against the fat shaming she sees as endemic in contemporary Western culture. Her message is both simple and radical: plus-sized people – especially plus-sized female people – have the right to live with dignity and respect.

Read's high online visibility has resulted in substantial media coverage as well as emotional greetings from strangers. Once, she was standing at an automatic teller machine when a woman came up and, in a sheepish-sounding voice, asked 'are you Fat Heffalump?'. When Read answered in the affirmative, the woman began crying before whispering, 'you've changed my life'. Hate, however, has also become part of daily life for Read:

> I can't ever remember using the internet and not getting shit … [Initially it] had nothing to do with my activism. I just happened to be the bearer of a vagina … If you're a woman and you say something … someone disagrees with … then – even without knowing what you look like – you're 'a fat bitch' or 'no man will have you' … I would be hard-pressed to find a woman who hasn't got it at some point. (K. Read, personal communication, 2 June 2015)

For Read, the 'fat, ugly, bitch' messages can arrive daily in their hundreds. People have also threatened to decapitate her with a chainsaw, and to smash her face in with a hammer if they see her in the street (cited in Elliott, 2016). Read keeps and files everything, partly because her librarian instinct is to collate, and partly because she wonders whether at some point it might be required as evidence in court.

Over the years, the drive-by abusers have been joined by (or have turned into) online stalkers. Specific individuals track Read's internet activity across various platforms, hunting for potential vulnerabilities and attempting to – in her words – 'pick the scabs off' anything that might cause her hurt. Read finds this 'way creepy', partly because she's never sure who or how many people she's dealing with. Her haters have also extended their efforts offline:

> Someone ... signed me up for every weight-loss clinic, gym, personal trainer, diabetes clinic ... in Brisbane ... They used the call centre number for my workplace ... [and] ... I was getting calls at work from quite innocent companies who were thinking that I had signed up to their thing. I was getting personal trainers and gyms and all sorts of [people] ringing me up [and saying], 'oh we believe you're in for bariatric surgery?' (K. Read, personal communication, 2 June 2015)

Removing herself from these databases took weeks of phone calls (Read cited in Elliott, 2016). Then there was the fall-out from the letters sent to her boss saying she should be sacked because she did not have the qualifications required for her position. Read's employers had sympathy for her situation and were outraged on her behalf. Her haters changed up again. One day, Read arrived home and found a note in her mailbox. It read: 'Hi fat bitch, I see this is where you live.'

Like most of the women I interviewed, Read does not like publicly admitting that the online 'shit' gets to her. In fact, a significant number of those women using their real names in my research asked me to redact from their transcripts any references they made to feeling frightened, anxious, distressed, and so on. Some don't want their attackers to know they had to take medication or see a psychiatrist in order to muster the strength to start leaving the house again. Others don't want these people to realise that, yes, actually they *are* quite sensitive about their skin condition, their weight, their parenting, their intelligence, their religion, that time they were raped, the death of their child... The concern is that attackers will know they have 'won' and may gain insights into how better to maximise distress in future. That said, staying schtum about the impact of cyberhate also represents a victory for assailants in that it silences women and invisibilises a significant gendered harm. It is also reminiscent of the toxic silence that surrounds offline sexual abuse.

Read is one of the few women I spoke to prepared to go on the record that she was, indeed, frightened when she found that note in her letterbox. As for tweets such as 'oh my god you are so ugly I wouldn't rape you'? They fill her with righteous anger, but can also feel like 'a smack in the face'. For her, constantly receiving such messages is, 'just like being vomited on every day ... it sticks to you'. She wants the world 'to know that this shit hurts and it affects our lives. It affects who we are' (K. Read, personal communication, 2 June 2015).

Especially words, especially the internet, especially women

As I will explain further in Chapters 4 and 5, commentators espousing the virtues of free speech often insist solving cyberhate is a cinch. Targets, they say, simply need to toughen up. The gist of their case relies on the old maxim about sticks and stones breaking bones but names never hurting. *It's only words, right?* Added to this is the contention that such hostility should not be taken seriously because it occurs in a virtual domain. *It's just the internet, yeah?* Related is the ongoing struggle to have verbal and physical violence against women recognised as hate speech and hate crime (see Angelari, 1993; Walters and Tumath, 2014; Maatz, 2015). In other words: *It's only women, after all...* My case, in contrast, is that gendered cyberhate is problematic *especially* because it involves the language of misogyny, *especially* because it's happening online, and *especially* because it targets women.

As discussed in the previous chapter, early thinking about cyberspace was dominated by the notion that there was a complete cleavage between the online and the offline. The utopian perspective was that the cybersphere should be celebrated as liberatory and novel, rather than regulated as potentially problematic or as yet another venue for old issues such as sexism and racism. Such beliefs reflected the libertarianism underpinning the development of the net. Now, at least in the privileged West, social media platforms and the internet are fully integrated in everyday life. We have to go out of our way to be other than always connected. As such, the concepts of 'being online' or 'being offline' have become anachronistic (Buchanan, 2011: 89). This is also reflected in government policies that have been implemented specifically to remove distinctions between online and offline identities and social relations. An example is the establishment of 'online participants as legal subjects with rights and responsibilities' in order to support the use of the internet for commerce and politics (Slater, 2002: 544).

Violence against women and girls is becoming similarly integrated in that attacks which begin online may spill offline, just as attacks which begin offline may subsequently involve online dimensions. Still other cases involve a combination of online and offline assaults from the outset. This chapter's examination of the impact of gendered cyberhate begins with those attacks which have a distinct offline component. This is not to imply that the cybersphere is something other than 'real' life or that certain attack contexts are automatically more serious or more likely to cause suffering than others. A knife-wielding stranger who turns up at a woman's house because her ex-partner has circulated a 'come rape me and my children' post in her name obviously represents a clear and present danger to the woman. That said, targets who are abused solely or primarily via internet channels also experience significant suffering, not least because many online threats are calculated so as to cause maximum fear about the possibility of offline events.

This chapter spells out the serious ramifications of gendered cyberhate. It looks at the online dimensions of offline domestic violence, as well as the consequences of mob attacks or 'dog-piles'[2], including *en masse* assaults that have been incited or otherwise facilitated by individuals (sometimes by high profile figures who make use of their large social media followings expressly for this purpose). The coercive force of gendered cyberhate is shown to cause emotional, social, financial, professional, and political harm, in that – among other impacts – it silences women, and constrains their ability to find jobs, market themselves, network, socialise, engage politically, and partake freely in self-expression and self-representation. Further, the harms caused by gendered cyberhate are shown to be *embodied* harms, giving lie to the idea that cyber violence can be dismissed as innocuous because it is entirely 'virtual'.

'Rape Me and My Daughters'

The practice of doxing – in which personally identifying information is published online to encourage and enable internet antagonists to hunt targets in the offline world – has the potential to cause women extreme fear and material harm. 'Feminista Jones' is the online pseudonym of an influential New York-based blogger and activist who identifies as a post-modern, sex-positive, Black feminist. She has been harassed by the holders of hundreds of social media accounts over a period of years, including attackers who painstakingly unearthed her offline identity, as well as her address and telephone number (Mantilla, 2015: 24–25). These were posted online along with her photograph and a call for people to approach her in public. The enthused respondents included a man who tweeted a photo he had taken of himself standing behind Jones and her son at an event (2015).

Such crowdsourced harassment is increasingly being observed as a dimension of domestic violence scenarios. For instance, men are publishing faux advertisements claiming their ex-wives or former girlfriends are soliciting sex (Jouvenal, 2013). One man posted an ad titled 'Rape Me and My Daughters' which included his ex-wife's home address and prompted more than 50 strangers to arrive at her home (Sandoval, 2013). This included one man who tried to break into the woman's home and another who attempted to undress her daughter (2013). In December 2009, meanwhile, a Wyoming woman was raped with a knife sharpener in her home after a former boyfriend assumed her identity online and posted a Craigslist notice that read, 'Need an aggressive man with no concern or regard for women' (2013).

The increasingly interconnected nature of 'traditional' domestic violence and cyber VAWG is a theme which emerged in my interview with Charley,[3] a woman who spoke via Skype from a women's refuge where she had lived for 10 months after escaping a situation of sustained domestic abuse. Charley reports being repeatedly raped by her former partner who had filmed these sexual assaults with her mobile phone. Shortly after police assisted her to flee her home, Charley's son alerted her to the fact that her former partner was posting threatening material about her on Facebook. She says these included posts reading 'fuck you bitch, fuck you whore', a picture of a toilet bowel full of faeces captioned with 'this is for you, you hungry piece of shit', and a photograph of an Iranian woman who had been executed by hanging after making claims of sexual assault against a man. Asked how it felt to have her son – and other friends and family – see these Facebook posts, Charley said she felt:

> Ashamed. Embarrassed. Humiliated … Him putting all this stuff on Facebook showed the world how little he thought of me. I wasn't able to hide it anymore. My shame now became public. I was being publicly humiliated. So this amazing woman, oh yeah she's a dog. She's a piece of shit. Look at her. (Charley, personal communication, 22 July 2015)

Concerned about what her former partner might do with the sexual assault footage he had collected, Charley says she spent an entire weekend searching revenge porn sites looking for videos of her rape. While she was unable to find anything, her concern is that it is just matter of time until they surface.

Similarly, a 2016 Australian government hearing into proposed revenge porn legislation heard the case of a young woman, known by the pseudonym 'Amira', who said she'd felt like a 'performing donkey' after her partner coerced her into sex with a sex worker, then posted images of the act on porn websites (Hasham, 2016). This woman said she feared her former partner would follow through on his threats to send the images to her family and friends if she did not do everything that he asked (2016). The stories of women such as Charley and Amira reveal the power of direct and indirect threats involving new technology, as well as the way 21st-century offenders are able to harness technology to extend their control over and intensify the suffering inflicted on their targets.

These anecdotal accounts are supported by empirical data such as that from the UK organisation Women's Aid, which has found that nearly half of women who suffer violence at the hands of a partner experience harassment or online abuse during their relationship as well as once they have left it, with 38 per cent of women being stalked online after they leave their partners (Smith, 2014). The criminologists Nicola Henry and Anastasia Powell observe that advances in technology are permitting the distribution of sexual assault images and enabling 'the continuation of harm ... well beyond the original crime'. Such acts reveal the extent to which 'multiple offenders are complicit in a wide range of sexually aggressive behaviors over and above the 'physical' act, including filming, watching, and distributing' (2015: 767). The academics Jenny Ostini and Susan Hopkins (2015) also draw attention to the extent to which new communication and surveillance technologies are increasingly being misused to stalk, intimidate, harass, humiliate, and coerce intimate partners, particularly girls and women. This includes: using electronic means to remove access to targets' bank account funds; blocking emails and phone calls from friends and family members; installing GPS trackers on targets' vehicles; and circulating false and/or intimate information about targets online (2015).

Another person I interviewed, Mary,[4] was 19 and had been with her boyfriend – an IT specialist – for about a year when he took exception to her plan to leave for a study abroad program in the US. As her departure date approached, Mary sent a routine email to her exchange coordinator who replied, confused, saying they had received an email from Mary the previous week officially withdrawing from the program. This email – sent from Mary's account without her knowledge – marked the beginning of a sustained, six-week effort to hijack her travel plans. This included sending emails on her behalf, as well as taking control of her email and Facebook accounts by changing her passwords. Mary started receiving messages sent to her from her own email address saying she would be raped and facially disfigured if she went through with her plans to travel to the US. She reports that one of these read:

> don't come over here, I'm going to hurt you, I'll enjoy raping you, you won't look the way you do after this … I can't wait to hear you scream in pain, I'll be waiting for you at the airport, you're going to have it … in every hole. (cited in personal communication, 10 September 2015)

These messages were copied in to study abroad program organisers in both Australia and the US. Mary says she considered cancelling her trip because she was frightened she would indeed be disfigured or killed. But her exchange coordinator urged her not to abandon her plans and arranged for a security detail to meet her at the airport in the US. Throughout all this, Mary was convinced – but did not have concrete proof – that the person behind this harassment was her now ex-boyfriend. Eventually she confronted him and promised not to pursue the matter with police if he agreed to delete her email and Facebook accounts. While her ex-boyfriend continued to deny having anything to do with the hacking, shortly after the conversation about alerting the police, both Mary's Facebook and email accounts were deleted as she had requested.

Revenge porn – often combined with doxing – is another increasingly common tactic used by women's ex-partners after relationship breakdowns. According to a 2015 Australian survey, one in 10 adults report having had a nude or semi-nude image of themselves posted online or sent to others without their permission (Powell and Henry, 2015a: 1). Danielle Keats Citron and Mary Anne Franks write of 'Jane', a nurse, whose ex-boyfriend posted a naked photo of her on a revenge porn site along with her contact details (2014). Jane received multiple emails, phone calls, and Facebook contacts from strangers, many of whom wanted sex. Yet the site refused to remove the photo and, even though the anonymous calls and emails were intensifying, police officers told Jane there was nothing they could do (Citron, 2014b).

Another emerging practice, 'sextortion', involves blackmailing targets in order to extort them to perform sexual acts online. In May 2016, the Brookings Institution compiled a list of 78 publicly available sextortion cases estimated to have involved up to 6500 possible victims (Wittes et al., 2016). Of the 78 cases focused on by researchers, 55 involved only victims who were minors, all the perpetrators were male, and nearly all the adult victims were female. Targets had been forced to record videos of themselves engaged in – among other acts – stripping, masturbating, having sex, and eating their own ejaculate. Offenders had obtained the original material used for blackmail by a range of techniques included hacking targets' computers and webcams, installing malware on their devices, or impersonating their boyfriends. One perpetrator, Luis Mijangos, was discovered with 15,000 webcam videos, 13,000 screen captures, and 900 audio recordings when the FBI confiscated his computers (Wittes et al., 2016: 12, 25, 2).

A case study demonstrating the integration of online and offline abuse involves the Australian psychology student Talitha Stone (2013b). In 2013, Stone was an activist aligned with Collective Shout, a morally conservative group which campaigns against 'the objectification of women and sexualisation of girls' ('Collective Shout', n.d.). Stone had launched a petition attempting to have the American rapper Tyler, the Creator denied a visa to enter Australia on the grounds that his pro-rape lyrics incited violence against women. When Tyler, the Creator tweeted news of Stone's further activism to his 1.7 million followers, it resulted in a barrage of rape and death threats targeting Stone and her family members (Lyons, 2014). In the midst of the Twitter-driven campaign against her, the rapper encouraged fans at a sold-out Sydney performance to cheer and pump their fists as he dedicated the song 'Bitch Suck Dick' to Stone, and said, 'Fucking bitch, I wish she could hear me call her a bitch, too, fucking whore. Yeah, I got a sold-out show right now bitch. Hey this fucking song is dedicated to you, you fucking cunt' (cited in Stone, 2013a). Stone was in the audience filming at the time and said she was petrified someone in the crowd would recognise her: 'I honestly didn't believe what I was hearing when he called me out. I was terrified' (cited in Lyons, 2014).

Coralie Alison,[5] a Collective Shout member who also launched a petition against Tyler, the Creator, was targeted by the rapper in 2015 when he falsely claimed she had caused him to be banned from Australia. His tweet read, 'T IS NOW BANNED FROM AUSTRALIA, YOU WON @ CoralieAlison IM HAPPY FOR YOU <3' and arrived in the feeds of a following that by then numbered 2.5 million (Di Stefano, 2015). The volume of tweets Alison received in response was so huge that she had to switch off the notifications function on her phone because the constant alerts were draining her battery:

> there was just a huge barrage of people describing ... how they wanted me to die, how they wanted me to suicide, what they personally were going to do to me ... they publicly said ... 'we have [your] address and we're coming to kill you' and things about my family, like about my niece, about my dad, stuff like 'I'm going to force your dad to rape you and make people watch' ... Someone had even found my personal Facebook account ... [and] had screen grabbed a whole family photo ... and then said 'they're all going to die'. (C. Alison, personal communication, 4 August 2015)

Stone and Alison's experiences show the way high profile figures are able to incite – either intentionally or otherwise – large fan bases to engage in mob attacks on named women. It also demonstrates that it doesn't matter whether a woman's politics are (for want of less reductive terms) socially progressive or morally conservative: the outrage provoked and the abuse received is the same.

Breaking points

A big part of the power of gendered cyberhate is its sheer relentlessness. For most targets, the abuse is not a one-off 'fuck you' they can delete and forget about. Instead, it arrives again and again, day in and day out via platforms essential for their work, and on devices they may be checking at home while they're watching cartoons with their kids, or lying in bed with their partners. On some days the messages may seem paint-dryingly tedious or even funny. Yet their cumulative impact can be debilitating. As Jessica Valenti puts it: 'You can't get called a cunt day in, day out for 10 years and not have that make a really serious impact on your psyche' (cited in Goldberg, 2015). As a result of the ongoing abuse, Valenti has stopped promoting her speaking events publicly and started hiring security (Hess, 2014). She feels like quitting her feminist activism 'all the time' (cited in Goldberg, 2015). Lindy West, too, describes the exhaustion of having 'everyone's poison just coming at you from all sides ... hundreds of people all day, every day' (cited in Mantilla, 2015: 41). West says she has become less trusting and outgoing: 'I feel like it's made my life smaller' (2015: 41).

This section of the book outlines the emotional and psychological fallout experienced by gendered cyberhate targets. While many participants in my project asked that information about their cyberhate-related distress (including some significant mental health diagnoses) be redacted, most granted permission for their experiences to be reported in a de-identified form. The following section, therefore, is based on my conversations with these women, as well as from material drawn from self-reports from cyberhate targets which have appeared elsewhere.

While the circumstances and reactions of female cyberhate targets vary, there are several commonalities. For instance, my research suggests that many recipients of such material demonstrate good humour and resilience in that quite often: (1) they are able to laugh off or ignore attacks; and (2) they feel angry and spurred to action, rather than beaten and cowed into silence. Thus caution should be exercised when using 'victim' language. The rise of various forms of feminist digilantism in response to misogyny online also show that many women are reclaiming a sense of power and agency by using a range of strategies to fight back against and sometimes enact revenge[6] on their male attackers (Jane, 2016a, 2016b, 2016c).

Despite this, however, most women I have interviewed admit they *have* reached one or more breaking points at which time their ability to cope has foundered or collapsed completely. This usually comes about as a result of: attacks which focus on subjects about which they are particularly sensitive (often involving family members); attacks which are particularly savage; and/or attacks which continue for very long periods and involve a very large number of messages. The burn-out associated with the latter is linked not only to the content of the material received, but also to the huge investment of time and energy required to block attackers, report individual instances of abuse to platforms, call police, attend court appearances, and so on. This dirty war is a dirty war of attrition.

The *Guardian* columnist Van Badham describes the immense fatigue she feels as the result of prolonged periods of being hunted online in ways which constantly raise the spectre of offline attacks. One man threatened to slit her throat at a political demonstration, while a Nazi site published her photograph and implored readers to run her down if they saw her. Then:

the other day, [a] packet of papers turned up in my house – my house! – with depictions of gang rapes and female genital mutilation, and the greatest of all threats unspoken: I know where you live. I've barely stayed the night there since. I'm moving soon. (Badham, 2015)

When gendered cyberhate targets reach breaking point, they describe emotional responses ranging from feelings of anxiety, sadness, shame, isolation, vulnerability, and unsafeness; to distress, pain, shock, fear, terror, and violation. Some report mental health problems such as anxiety disorder, depression, panic attacks, agoraphobia, and self-harm. Sensational 'death by social media' headlines about cyberbullies causing targets to suicide should obviously be taken with a grain of salt, given the radical unknowability of where correlation ends and causation begins in such cases. That said, cyberhate targets with pre-existing mental health conditions are decidedly vulnerable, especially when attackers incite suicide – which attackers tend to do if a target is known to be struggling with mental illness. Young queers are at particular risk. American statistics show that 45 per cent of school-aged lesbian, gay, bisexual, or transgender (LGBT) cyber harassment targets feel depressed, and more than 25 per cent wrestle with suicidal thoughts (Citron, 2014a: 11). Cyberbullying and sexual humiliation online – including the posting of sexual assault images – have also been linked to a number of teenagers who have taken their own lives (see: Citron, 2014a: 11, 149, 188; Mantilla, 2015: 13–14).

A case study from Australia in 2012 involves the depressed TV presenter Charlotte Dawson who was hospitalised after receiving a barrage of messages such as: 'Freedom of speech, you fucking bimbo? Go kill yourself'; 'I speak for everyone in the universe. Bitch, you need to kill yourself'; and 'Go kill yourself you fucking whore' (cited in Brown, 2012). Dawson was still engaging with her online attackers – tweeting 'Hope this ends the misery' and 'You win' – only an hour before an ambulance was called to her home in Sydney because of a suicide attempt (Colvin and Mark, 2012; Brown, 2012). Eighteen months later, the former *Australia's Next Top Model* judge took her own life. While a consideration of Dawson's mental health in general terms is obviously relevant, it is difficult to avoid the conclusion that her online experiences were intimately bound up with her self-destructive behaviour as proximate if not ultimate causes.

Pre-existing psychiatric conditions are not, however, necessary for women to suffer tremendously from gendered cyberhate. Indeed, some targets with otherwise robust mental health report developing debilitating psychological problems in the aftermath of abuse. On the day the attacks against Criado-Perez were at their worst, for example, she says she 'broke down completely, utterly overwhelmed' because she thought it would never end:

> By this point, it had been going on for a week ... I struggled to eat, to sleep, to work. I lost about half a stone in a matter of days. I was exhausted and weighed down by carrying these vivid images, this tidal wave of hate around with me wherever I went ... The psychological fall-out is still unravelling. I feel like I'm walking around like a timer about to explode; I'm functioning at just under boiling point – and it takes so little to make me cry – or to make me scream. (2013)

Consider, too, the huge emotional (and financial) cost and disruption to life that occurs if a woman feels she must suddenly leave her home in order to protect her safety. During GamerGate, Brianna Wu remembers watching a stash of her personal details suddenly appear online during an attack:

> I was literally watching the chat room as the site posted my address and the conversation moved to places that threatened my personal safety. I made the decision to leave, and law enforcement said it was reasonable. I basically just left the house. I have no idea where I'll be living this week or even next month. (cited in Stuart, 2014a)

Part of the force of gendered cyberhate – and this relates to the ambiguity of its online/offline status – is that it is impossible for targets to know whether a threat is credible. This can result in feelings of paranoia, as well as anxiety-producing states of hyper-vigilance. Valenti, for instance, says that whenever a male stranger approaches her at a public event, the hairs on the back of her neck stand on end (cited in Hess, 2014). Holli Thometz, a US woman targeted for a particularly virulent campaign based around revenge porn and doxing, became so fearful she bought a stun gun, changed her name to Holly Jacobs, and withdrew from online activities (Citron, 2014a: 46, 48). As she said:

> I just feel like I'm now a prime target for actual rape. I never walk alone at night, and I get chills when I catch someone staring at me. I always wonder to myself, 'Are they staring at me because they recognize me from the Internet?' (cited in Citron, 2014: 48)

Targets of gendered cyberhate often berate themselves for both overreacting (*it's just words, it's just the internet*) as well as underreacting (*but what if that rapey dude* does *show up at the house and one of the kids answers the door?*). The high levels of sexual and other types of violence against women in offline contexts give online rape threats extra punch, adding to the ambience of fear and powerlessness experienced by those who feel that sexual violence is an evitable fact of life. In this way gendered cyberhate can be seen as being both a manifestation of and contributing factor to what is known as 'rape culture' (Buchwald et al., 1993).

Reflecting back over the accounts given by women in this section, it is revealing to observe the physicality of the language such as that used by Read (cyberhate is like vomit), Valenti (the hairs on her neck stand on end), and Thometz/Jacobs (she gets chills). This illustrates the way seemingly disembodied discourse online can have an embodied impact. Many of my interviewees describe their experiences online in physical terms (for example: 'it felt like being kicked in the guts', 'it felt like being slapped in the face')[7], as well as reporting physical manifestations such as increased heartbeat, sweating, feelings of nausea, and so on. This raises the contentious topic of whether online attacks should only ever be categorised as virtual and disembodied, or whether they constitute harms that can manifest in bodies.

For Henry and Powell, technological-facilitated sexual violence (TFSV) involves physical, emotional, symbolic, and/or structural violence, whose harms can be located on a continuum of violence ranging from choice to pressure to coercion to force (2015: 759). These may be clearly serious criminal offences or unlawful civil harms, or they may be neither unlawful nor criminal, depending on the jurisdiction (2015: 759–60). Henry and Powell's case is that law, policy, and scholarly research orientations are obfuscating the extent to which the harms experienced by women in the sociospatial world are not disembodied, but may have at least as much impact on a person as traditional harms occurring against the physical body (2015: 760, 765).

Henry and Powell's argument is informed in part by feminist theories of the embodied subject (2015: 765). Recent advances in neurophysiology and cellular biology, however, make it possible to reject any remaining shreds of Cartesian mind-body dualism without recourse to philosophy, feminist theory, or anecdotal accounts of the embodied sensations associated with putatively non-physical attacks. While terms such as 'harm' and 'injury' are understood and applied very differently in the natural sciences, it is now understood that cognition, emotion, and social context can be even more influential than tissue damage in terms of producing physical pain (Moseley, 2007; Moseley, 2011; Moseley et al., 2012; Butler and Moseley, 2013). Note that these findings do not refer to sensations that feel *similar* to physical pain, or are *on par with* physical pain psychologically or morally, but are *exactly* physical pain.

The discovery that pain is first and foremost a brain event rather than a tissue event seems Copernican in its revolutionariness. Moreover, the 'medicosociolegal' nature of the modern world (Moseley et al., 2012: 37) means such findings are likely to become increasingly relevant in a growing number of contexts, particularly those involving considerations of harms or injuries that are not visible to the naked eye or apparent in medical scans. Certainly this research is already on the radar of the legal profession (Davis, 2016). While it is beyond the scope of this book to discuss these matters in greater detail, we must at least acknowledge the way they seriously complicate the ability to make neat distinctions between embodied injuries that cause physical pain and disembodied injuries that cause what are usually regarded as different and/or lesser sorts of suffering.

Dropping zeroes

Skepticism is a common response to those who say they suspect that large groups of hostile strangers are plotting their downfall. In the gendered cyberhate scene, however, such beliefs are not just baseless conspiracy theorising. Brianna Wu reports finding GamerGate threads on Reddit, 8chan, and 4chan initiated 'to discredit and destroy' her (cited in Stuart, 2014a). Many of the public figures I interviewed for my research report finding similar threads in similar venues in which groups discuss how best to attack them, destroy their reputations, cause them distress, and so on.

Organised attempts to undermine or end people's livelihoods are one of the reasons many cyberhate targets suffer economically and professionally. In her advocacy work on sexism in cyberspace, the Massachusetts congresswoman Katherine Clark (2015) makes the point that online threats cost real money through missed wages, legal fees, and private protection services. She notes that the average cost for an instance of cyberstalking is US$1200, and that this is a cost disproportionately born by women (2015). Women who withdraw from the internet or dramatically scale down their online engagement also pay a price in dollar terms. Cyberhate targets may lose productivity (Jane – the nurse targeted for revenge porn – did not go to work for days), or may lose their jobs altogether (Citron, 2014b). In addition to those women subject to campaigns to have them fired (Doyle, 2011c), others are effectively tormented into unemployment and obscurity. At the time Sierra was hounded off the internet in 2007, for instance, she gave up book deals and speaking engagements – key components of her career in tech (Sandoval, 2013). These stories show the way gendered cyberhate can be seen as constituting a new form of workplace harassment that – thanks to the 'always on' culture of contemporary employment – often extends well beyond the office.

Online abuse has the power to destroy women's reputations in ways which have significant and ongoing repercussions for their future employment prospects. Findings from the Pew Research Center show that of those people targeted for physical threats and sustained harassment, about a third feel their reputations have been damaged (Duggan, 2014: 7). Citron's (2014b) work shows that schools have fired teachers whose naked photos have appeared on revenge porn sites, while a government agency terminated a woman's employment after a co-worker circulated her nude photograph to colleagues. Cogent, too, is the fact that most employers rely on candidates' online reputation to filter applicants. Nearly 80 per cent of employers consult search engines to collect intelligence on job applicants, and about 70 per cent of applicants are rejected because of these findings (Citron, 2014c). Common reasons for not interviewing and hiring applicants include concerns about 'lifestyle', 'inappropriate' online comments, and 'unsuitable' photographs, videos, and information. As Citron puts it:

> The simple but regrettable truth is that after consulting search results, employers don't call revenge porn victims to schedule an interview or to extend offers. It's just seen as good business to avoid hiring people whose search results would reflect poorly on them. (2014b)

The female cultural critics, journalists, and game developers attacked by GamerGaters are particularly exposed economically because they are engaged in what is known as 'precarious' labour (Elliot, 2015). The sociologist Amanda Elliot's observation is that many of the laws and institutional provisions that emerged to provide (albeit limited) protection to women from sexual harassment in the Fordist workplace provide little to no protection in the new economy (2015). Her point about precarious labour comports with the experiences of many of the women I interviewed. For them, work is unpredictable, eclectic, and self-driven. As such, blogging, social media influence, online visibility, and the promotion of their personal 'brands' are key to their livelihoods (as well as being core elements of the way they conduct their political activism, and maintain their social support networks). One of my interviewees, an independent filmmaker, says she is no longer able to rely on a key industry website used by her international peers to network and crowdsource funds because of a harassment campaign against her on the site.

Dealing with cyberhate is also time-consuming. As the US writer Amanda Hess (2014) puts it, 'Every time we call the police, head to court to file a civil protection order, or get sucked into a mental hole by the threats that have been made against us, zeroes drop from our annual incomes'. Even dealing with cyberhate as an ally of targets is time-consuming. Alison, for instance, says that, during the attack by fans of Tyler, the Creator, some of her supporters filled out online forms reporting individual messages to Twitter for six hours straight on her behalf. One woman joked that she'd developed carpal tunnel syndrome from so many hours of reporting, because each individual report she filed required 10 mouse clicks.

The dark arts of silencing

Activists often argue that gendered cyberhate is being deployed by men in an attempt to silence women – a reading supported by the imagery in messages such as, 'IF THIS TRASH TALKING K*NT HAD HER F*CKNG, TONGUE RIPPED OUT OF HER SUCK-HOLE ...' (cited in Lewis, 2011). From an academic perspective, however, difficulties arise in terms of locating evidence to support the silencing thesis, in that one must prove the absence rather than the presence of a thing. This is extremely hard if not outright impossible. And can a woman who says she has been silenced by gendered cyberhate really be considered silenced if she is speaking about the problem to a journalist or an academic?

When I was conducting my interviews, a number of women spoke of female friends or colleagues who had withdrawn from all online engagement (including email) after cyberhate attacks. I sent messages – via my interviewees – to these 'disappeared' women, asking if they would speak to me anonymously or even off the record. All refused – which may be regarded as some form of evidence that this kind of overt, absolute silencing does occur. There are also media reports about feminist activists who have completely abandoned their online presence in order to avoid the 'toxic stew' (Lauren Bruce cited in Goldberg, 2015).

Without wishing to underplay or ignore these sorts of experiences, my overall conclusion is that it is rare for silencing to occur in an all-or-nothing fashion. Instead, it is more common for women to be silenced in some ways and in some contexts, but not in others. For instance, many of my subjects said they would have censored sections of the accounts they gave me if they had been unable to use pseudonyms for all or part of their interviews. Others reflected back on periods where they had withdrawn for periods of time from the cybersphere. Thus a person may feel metaphorically voiceless at one point but not another. As such, it is not useful to think about silencing in absolute terms in that a woman is *entirely* vocal or *entirely* mute the *entire* time. Instead, as with emerging theoretical work on digital divides[8] (see Van Dijk and Hacker, 2003; Van Deursen and Van Dijk, 2014), the most helpful approach is to examine overall patterns in internet use from an equity perspective.

An insidious type of silencing involves women changing the style or content of their work in anticipation of cyberhate. Joan Walsh (2007) – who says she has had to metaphorically armour-up in a way she does not like – notes the way women writers reflexively compose their own hate mail in their minds as they write, sometimes typing and re-typing their work in the hope of pre-emptively avoiding it. While Walsh feels this has made her more precise and less glib, she says it has also muted her writing and made her overly cautious (2007). My case is that there exists a strong link between gendered cyberhate and decisions to self-censor and/or to avoid a range of topics and debates expected to attract abuse. These decisions are being made either because women have been personally attacked in similar circumstances previously, or because they have witnessed such attacks on others.

Almost all my interviewees volunteered a list of hashtags they say they will never use again because doing so brings down a rain of hate: #gamergate is at the top of nearly everyone's list. Relevant, here, are the experiences of the US actress and gamer Felicia Day who, in November 2014, confessed that she had been silent on the subject of GamerGate because she was frightened of being attacked and doxed by members of the culture she loves:

> I have been terrified of inviting a deluge of abusive and condescending tweets into my timeline. I did one simple @ reply to one of the main victims several weeks back, and got a flood of things I simply couldn't stand to read directed at me. I had to log offline for a few days until it went away. I have tried to retweet a few of the articles I've seen dissecting the issue in support, but personally I am terrified to be doxxed for even typing the words 'Gamer Gate' ... I have allowed a handful of anonymous people to censor me. (2014)

Apparently Day was doxed within minutes of this piece being published (Hern, 2014). The former NFL player Chris Kluwe used Day's experience to highlight the differing treatment meted out to women as opposed to men who speak publicly about GamerGate. 'None of you fucking #gamergate tools tried to dox me, even after I tore you a new one ...' he tweeted. 'Instead, you go after a woman who wrote why your movement concerns her' (cited in Hern, 2014). (Kluwe (2014) had previously called GamerGaters 'angry neckbeards', 'paint-hugging shitgoblins', 'slopebrowed weaseldicks', 'basement-dwelling, cheetos-huffing, poop-sock-sniffing douchepistol[s]', 'slackjawed pickletits', and 'hemorrhoidal gunt stains'.)

Another silencing-related issue concerns not just whose voices are missing but whose continue to be heard. For example, debates about contentious topics may become dominated by women whose politics are avowedly non-social justice related, whose views align with those of male cyberhaters, who have the financial resources to hire adequate online and offline security, who have very secure employment, and/or whose skins are so thick they are unmoved by rape and death threats. (This is not to criticise such women; merely to identify potential patterns.) Conversely, women who are emotionally affected by cyberhate, who have precarious jobs they do not wish to jeopardise, who can't afford or don't know how to secure adequate online or offline protection, and/or who have children or other family members they wish to protect may withdraw. Thus the full spectrum of views on a given topic may not be heard, potentially resulting in larger changes to debate cultures and democratic citizenship online. Lindy West (2015), for instance, warns of a world where public discourse is (even more) dominated by white, heterosexual, able-bodied men. Valenti adds that, as a frequent guest speaker at colleges, young women often tell her they would like to be writers but are choosing other vocations because they don't have the stomach for the abuse:

This is especially true for women of colour and trans women: we are losing out on talented writers who are part of marginalised communities because they don't want to pursue a career where harassment is considered an expected part of the gig. (2016)

Jill Filipovic, a senior political writer covering feminist issues at *Cosmopolitan*, reports recently trying to persuade a friend to run for political office. Her friend replied: 'There's several reasons why I wouldn't want to do it, but one of them is that I follow you on Twitter, and I see what people say to you. I could never deal with that' (cited in Goldberg, 2015).

Silencing also occurs when women feel unable to speak about being threatened online because of the fear this will provoke yet more abuse. Again, the reasoning here is entirely rational. The list of women who have spoken openly about being attacked only to suffer even more assaults (including offline variations) is a long one. As previously discussed, gendered e-bile exposure often leads to gendered e-bile amplification. Women also say they are reluctant to speak out because they don't want to be accused of lacking humour, of being weak or thin-skinned, of being opposed to the principles of free speech, or of being typecast as 'whiners' (see Lewis, 2011; Evans, 2011; Penny, 2011). All these tendencies are likely to contribute to the underreporting of cyber violence discussed in Chapter 5.

Related to the notion of silencing in speech-related contexts are those situations where women's identity and self-expression is oppressively restricted. An example involves female gamers playing as male characters in an attempt to slip beneath the radar of attackers. One of my interviewees, a 24-year-old gamer, doesn't just adopt male avatars and user names, she uses voice modulating software so as to sound male when using voice-initiated video games:

You can calibrate a voice modulator however you want. I take the high pitch and transfer it to a lower pitch so that my whole voice sounds much more masculine. It's what I do when I really couldn't be arsed dealing with the hate. (personal communication, 18 June 2015)

This is far from the sort of playful identity construction lauded by early, cyberutopian visions of the freedoms permitted by the internet. It is a deliberate decision by a woman to entirely elide her gender so as to avoid abuse.

A different but related phenomenon involves those of my interviewees who say they now refrain from posting not only sexualised images of themselves, but *any* images of themselves in public fora online. These women restrict themselves to displaying what they see as 'safe' pictures – often of pets, restaurant meals, or natural landscapes, and never of children or family members. Indeed, many female cyberhate targets say circulating any information of a personal nature has become too risky. From a feminist perspective, it would be concerning if women began feeling less comfortable sharing stories that have traditionally been dismissed as 'women's business' and relegated to the private domestic sphere. Cooking, cleaning, caring for new, old, or unwell humans ... feminists have battled long and hard to have these aspects of life rendered visible, to have women's unpaid work in these areas acknowledged, and to advocate for more equitable load-sharing between the genders. That some women are feeling it necessary to erase these parts of their lives from the public cybersphere is a backward step.

Further, these changes in internet use are not trivial or minor. The term 'web 2.0' – also referred to as the 'read-write' web (Lessig, 2007) – refers to cumulative alterations in the way the web has been constructed and accessed such that user-generated content, interactivity, collaboration, and sharing is emphasised. This is in contrast to the 'web 1.0' period where the internet was in mostly a static, read-only format. When women truncate and censor their self-expression and self-representation online, or adopt a 'broadcast' model of communication, their usage styles hark back to a 1.0 rather than a 2.0 model of web use. In theory, they are still able to operate as interactive content producers. In practice, however, this is something they approach with extreme caution. Many of my interviewees, for instance, report disabling comments on their blogs or 'locking down' their social media presence so as to avoid interactions with strangers – including strangers who might represent potential networking and collaboration opportunities. Thus some of the most celebrated aspects of the web 2.0 era – self-publishing, engagement, interaction, collaboration, and interoperability – are no longer as readily available because continuing to access them involves untenably high costs. In short, women are having to use the internet equivalent of an antiquated computer operating system.

Coercion

It could be argued that women who opt out of some conversations, who avoid certain, most, or all online venues, and/or who post only photos of their Reuben sandwiches or Miniature Schnauzers are making free decisions rather than being gagged or coerced. There is good evidence, however, that gendered cyberhate does constitute a form of coercion and, as such, is undermining women's autonomy and freedom. In philosophy, the term 'hard choice' is used to describe a choice situation in which rejecting a proposal puts one in dire straits, but accepting the proposal is also unpalatable (Wertheimer, 1987: 233). Thus, for Alan Wertheimer, 'the family of coercion terms' can be plausibly used to describe hard choice situations (1987: 233). Such hard choice scenarios are relevant to the legal defense of duress which applies to situations in which a person of 'reasonable firmness' is unable to resist a threat and is therefore coerced into a course of action (Morse, 2009: 268–9). Writing on the freedom-undermining effects of indoctrination and coercion, Gideon Yaffe offers the coercive scenario of a robber holding a gun to the head of an employee with a key to the cash:

> A cashier who coolly and calmly calculates the gains and losses of defiance and chooses to comply is no less a victim of coercion … The cashier is as free to herself as any of us are when we make a decision in favor of self-interest, but she is not, nonetheless, free. (2003: 341)

By the same token, a gendered cyberhate target may voluntarily withdraw from Twitter or Facebook after coolly and calmly calculating the gains and losses of the move. Yet she may still have been coerced. She makes a choice to withdraw, and her choice is rational, but she has still been coerced because coercion involves the illegitimate manipulation of situations and options in order to change what it is rational for another person to choose. Following Yaffe, my case is that manipulators in the form of misogynist cyber-antagonists are limiting women's opportunities online in ways neutral causal forces do not – 'and it is that sense in which manipulators take away from our freedom' (Yaffe, 2003: 344). Regardless of what some media commentators might claim, gendered cyberhate is not a feature of the natural environment like a tornado or an earthquake. It is produced by people, and that makes it legitimate to object when those people put women in a situation where withdrawing from the public cybersphere or greatly curtailing their internet use becomes the most rational choice for them to make.

A potential objection to the coercion argument is the frequently voiced claim that online threats are not 'real' threats because their senders do not intend to carry them out (more on this in Chapter 4). It could be argued, therefore, that the position women find themselves in online does not constitute a true hard choice scenario. My response is that, yes, it is, indeed, impossible to know whether online threats are credible threats. But this is precisely the reason they carry such force. Women cannot divine the inner machinations of online antagonists. As such, they are left wondering, 'what if this is the one time a man *does* do what he is threatening to do?' Given that cyber abuse tends to arrive *en masse*, women know that, even if the vast majority of men threatening rape, mutilation or death have no intention of following through, one non-empty threat is all it would take. Women *have* been physically assaulted as a result of online attacks that have spilled offline. It is entirely rational, therefore, to entertain the possibility that one of the multitude of antagonists might well follow through and attempt to harm them physically in an offline situation.

Jean Baudrillard's (2001) work on simulacra and simulation also assists in showing that whether threats against women are 'real' or 'not real' is not only epistemically unknowable, but largely irrelevant given their function as signs. In his essay on 'offensive simulation' and the 'impossibility of staging an illusion', Baudrillard also uses the analogy of a hold-up:

> How to feign a violation and put it to the test? ... Go and simulate a theft in a large department store ... Be sure to check that your weapons are harmless, and take the most trustworthy hostage, so that no life is in danger ... Demand ransom, and arrange it so that the operation creates the greatest commotion possible. In brief, stay close to the 'truth', so as to test the reaction of the apparatus to a perfect simulation. But you won't succeed: the web of artificial signs will be inextricably mixed up with real elements (a police officer will really shoot on sight; a bank customer will faint and die of a heart attack; they will really turn the phoney ransom over to you). In brief, you will unwittingly find yourself immediately in the real... (2001: 180–1)

By the same token, the question of whether a gendered cyberhate threat is 'authentic' or otherwise becomes irrelevant. For cyberhate targets – as with the occupants of the department store in Baudrillard's hold-up analogy – the web of the simulation or the parody becomes inextricably combined with the real. This is the reason a threat's reality status may have little impact on its 'efficiency'[9] *as* a threat. Also consider bomb threats made to schools and businesses. Whether the bomb is there or not, perpetrators of the threat are pursued and punished. Making the threat is recognised as an offence in itself. Perhaps the difference is that bomb threats are a public nuisance which disrupts organisations and not just women in the private realm.[10]

When the multiple and serious harms of gendered cyberhate are acknowledged, it is clear that this discourse wields a coercive force that is hurting – and digitally disenfranchising – its targets. Some women are being silenced, while others are paying a dreadful price in order to continue speaking. Further, not every individual who uses the internet need be attacked in order to suffer the chilling force of misogyny online. Female users who witness others being abused are changing their online engagement in an attempt to avoid similar harassment themselves. The vigilance women are exercising around self-censorship online is reminiscent of the effect of a panopticon in that they feel under constant surveillance and self-monitor accordingly. In Jeremy Bentham's original proposal for a jail in which prisoners had to assume they were always being observed, the panopticon's surveillants were authorised representatives of the state. In the case of gendered cyberhate, however, the guard tower is manned by hostile forces while – as we will see in Chapter 5 – the policing powers-that-be are busy asking cyber stalking victims, 'What is Twitter?'

Notes

1 Read was one of my interview subjects. All quotes from her are drawn from our interview, unless referenced otherwise.
2 'Dog-pile' is a slang term for an intense attack, often involving mobs, on an individual online.
3 'Charley' is a pseudonym.
4 'Mary' is a pseudonym.
5 I interviewed Alison as part of my cyberhate study.
6 This is not to endorse either the ethics or efficacy of digilante tactics.
7 Many thanks to Melanie Andersen for observing this aspect of interviewees' stories.
8 'Digital divide' is a term used to discuss online equity. It refers to differences between population groups in terms of the access and use of information and communications technologies.
9 For a discussion of the 'efficiency' of threats see Glukhov and Martynova, 2015: 62.
10 Many thanks to Melanie Andersen for input here.

4

THE BLAME GAME

The princesses all need to man up

In 2012, I delivered a keynote at a public seminar organised by an Australian university. During this talk I mentioned that my previous media work had meant spending many years waking to an in-box full of anonymous rape threats. Another invited speaker, a professor far more senior than myself, spoke up to explain (some might say 'mansplain') that the real problem was not the material I had received but my reaction to it. His public advice to me was to suggest I develop some resilience (because apparently continuing to write a weekly column through a 14-year rape-threat-a-palooza was not resilience enough). His final words of wisdom were: 'Toughen up, princess.'

The targets of gendered cyberhate are well used to such counsel. Media pundits, other internet users, and yes, even academics, have accused women who complain about online abuse of being too sensitive, too humourless, too hysterical, too princessy, and so on. Even Joan Walsh (2007), the former *Salon* writer referred to in earlier chapters, recalls telling female colleagues upset by cyberhate to 'man up', even though sometimes she knew her reaction amounted to telling them to stop wearing such provocative outfits online lest they got what they deserved.

In this chapter, I show the many ways women are blamed for gendered cyberhate, while men are exculpated. While the most flagrant examples of this occur in media commentary, as I will show in Chapter 5, the blame women/ excuse men dynamic is clearly evident in the actions and non-actions of institutions. There is good evidence, therefore, that the blatant victim-blaming around gendered cyberhate in media narratives is representative of a view held by many in non-media positions of power. This chapter also shows the way discourse around gendered cyberhate often has a paradoxical dimension in that the internet is framed as both tacky and trivial (on par with a video game console in that ceasing to play is an easy and consequence-free choice) *as well as* exotic and inherently terribly dangerous (on par with a potentially deadly natural environment like an uncharted wilderness or a high altitude zone of the Himalayas).

'A Victorian lady faints upon receiving a rude telegram' – women are blamed

Most critics of women who complain about misogyny online invoke arguments relating to free speech. The claim is that restricting online expression in any way is an untenable and dangerous form of censorship, and that letting all voices, including the most hateful and threatening ones, circulate freely is the lesser evil. One senior tech writer even argues that legislating against revenge porn poses an unacceptable threat to free speech (see Riley, 2015). My response to arguments based on appeals to the ideals of free speech can be found in the next chapter.

One of the most infamous (and decidedly troll-like) commentators on this subject is the internationally syndicated columnist Brendan O'Neill (2015), who has argued – in relation to the imprisonment of Isabella Sorley and John Nimmo over the online abuse of Caroline Criado-Perez – that jailing people for being offensive is a greater moral ill than posting threats on the internet. Writing in support of GamerGaters, O'Neill claims that fantasising about or role-playing the killing or beating of women is not problematic, but represents 'a central part of the freedom of the mind, which is the very backbone of freedom itself' (O'Neill, 2014). In stark contrast with these lady-slaying freedom fighters are 'Victim Feminists' who, 'having cleansed the public realm of offensive ideas ... now want to cleanse men's very souls' (2014). O'Neill denounces women concerned about rape threats and other online abuse as 'fragile', 'hilarious', 'delicate', 'peculiarly sensitive', Orwellian, and on par with Victorian ladies who fainted upon receiving a rude telegram or having heard men use coarse language (O'Neill, 2011). Such women, he says, are also guilty of the anti-Enlightenment crime of muddying 'the historic philosophical distinction between words and actions', and are hell bent on turning the internet into the online equivalent of 'a Women's Institute meeting, where no one ever raises their voice' (2011).

Similar views are offered by the commentator Ian O'Doherty (2015), who ridicules those offended by Twitter as suffering 'a fit of the vapours' and 'retreating into a position of squawking victimhood' every time they receive an 'unpleasant message'. Continuing the theme of hysterical irrationality is the UK columnist Patrick West (2015), who says online death and rape threats are not likely to be 'real, sincere or authentic' because people who actually intend to carry out such acts do not announce them in public. Proper psychopaths, he explains, are too clever and calculated to be so cavalier (2015). (Presumably West missed the Southern Poverty Law Center report showing that racist killers do not hide in the shadows but openly advocate their ideology online, often obsessively posting on forums and blogs for hours a day (Beirich, 2014).) West's position is that Twitter is not reality, and that, 'Those who talk imperiously about imaginary death threats are mostly grandstanding ... the latest manifestation of our society's predilection for narcissistic victimhood'. The UK actor Steven Berkoff, meanwhile, comes right out with it:

> There's a lot of talk about people being abused on Twitter, women being savagely insulted and degraded. I think, why get into that in the first place? If I jump into a garbage bin, I can't complain that I've got rubbish all over me. (cited in Cavendish, 2013)

Victim blaming in relation to gendered cyberhate is not only rife, but multi-layered. In the UK, Mary Beard, a professor of classics at Cambridge University, was targeted by the (now defunct) web site *Don't Start Me Off!* in 2013 after she appeared on a BBC television program disagreeing with claims that an influx of immigrants was making parts of England seem like 'a foreign country' (Stevens, 2013). Contributors to *Don't Start Me Off!* discussed plots to 'plant a dick' in Beard's mouth and rape her; speculated about the length of her pubic hair and the capaciousness of her vagina; and superimposed an image of her face onto female genitalia (Beard, 2013; Graham and Henry, 2013). Reflecting on this 'internet fury', Beard noted that, 'the misogyny here is truly gobsmacking [and] ... more than a few steps into sadism. It would be quite enough to put many women off appearing in public, contributing to political debate' (Beard, 2013). In response, the co-owner and moderator of the website, the Kent-based businessman Richard White, gave a qualified apology to Beard, but insisted that *Don't Start Me Off!* was a 'humour site' rather than a 'hate site' (cited in Dowell, 2013). He suggested the real troll might be Beard because she had encouraged her friends and colleagues to bombard *Don't Start Me Off!* with Latin poetry which he did not have time to translate (Dowell, 2013). White said Beard should have known better than to enter the 'self-contained', bantering, pub-style community of *Don't Start Me Off!*: 'She came to us by Googling us and in a sense looking for negative comments. We never went to her' (Dowell, 2013).

A common contention is that women are choosing to be upset by online aggression and can solve the problem simply by exercising their free will and choosing not to be upset. The American troll Jason Fortuny, for instance, says the willingness of targets to be hurt by words makes them complicit in the problem and trolling will end just as soon as they get over it (cited in Schwartz, 2008). Similar assertions are made in academic contexts. Richard MacKinnon, for instance, argues that a notorious virtual rape committed in the online community LambdaMOO in 1993 provides theoreticians with the opportunity to re-analyse rape as a mutable social construction, in a way which could alleviate pain, stigmatization, and victimization (MacKinnon, 1997). His idea is that virtual rapees consider removing the 'sex' from sexual assault by decoding or recoding their violated anatomy (MacKinnon, 1997). While he acknowledges the suggestion is controversial and the undertaking difficult, MacKinnon believes this approach might even be imported off-line. The trick seems to be to recode penises, anuses, and vaginas as being more on par with, say, fingers, ears, and noses, so that victims of sexual assault become victims of assault only, thereby experiencing 'little if any social repercussions' (MacKinnon, 1997). While MacKinnon's aim to reduce rape survivors' suffering is commendable, the idea that a man who hurts a woman's vagina during coerced sex might be recoded so as to be more akin to a man who hurts another man's elbow during a pub brawl is dubious to say the least.

The anecdotal accounts of victim-blaming discussed above are part of a much broader pattern. The UN Broadband Commission, for instance, cites figures indicating that nearly a quarter of women are blamed for the violence done to them online and argues that interventions must 'aggressively address and attack' this 'destructive response' ('Cyber violence against women and girls: A world-wide wake-up call', 2014: 22, 30). I concur. Blaming the targets of gendered cyberhate is unjust and cruel in that it inflicts further punishment on girls and women who have already suffered.

Further, the subtext of the victim-blaming rhetoric goes beyond 'you were asking for it', and extends to, 'oh, and since you were the ones who brought all this internet hate on yourselves, it's up to you and the rest of the squawking princesses to solve the problem' (a task we might be able to get round to once we've finished re-coding our vaginas as men's elbows). As with offline sexual harassment and violence, women are being counselled to stop engaging in the internet versions of getting too drunk, of flirting with the wrong men, of wearing rape-friendly clothing, of walking home through the wrong neighbourhoods, and so on. Those in power are dragging their feet with regards to prevention, redress, and victim support, while the *real* reason for rape threats – the men who make them – are often conspicuously absent from the gendered cyberhate conversation. Apparently these lucky fellows don't have to change a thing. Which is just as well because, as we will see, apparently asking them to change would be like asking snow to stop being cold.

'If you go on to the computer without your clothes on, you'll catch a virus' – men are excused

We have already seen the way women are dehumanised (Lindy West's (2013b) term is 'treated like subhuman garbage') via gendered cyberhate. Interestingly enough, much discourse about online hostility also relieves men of their personhood – although in a manner that benefits rather than harms them. This occurs partly via the aforementioned focus on female targets' putatively problematic online behaviour (which sidelines or invisibilises the fact that some actual attackers may have been involved). It also occurs when the internet is framed as a place that is inherently dangerous rather than a place where some humans go and commit harmful deeds. Consider the following comments made by Australia's federal police assistant commissioner, Shane Connelly, to a 2016 government inquiry about whether new laws were required to address revenge porn. Connelly's view is that:

> People just have to grow up in terms of what they're taking and loading on to the computer because the risk is so high … [They say] if you go out in the snow without clothes on you'll catch a cold – if you go on to the computer without your clothes on, you'll catch a virus. (cited in '"Grow up" and stop taking naked photos of yourself, police tell revenge porn inquiry', 2016)

Connelly's position frames the internet not just as intrinsically dangerous, but as intrinsically dangerous in the same way a blizzard or a region susceptible to earthquakes is dangerous. The cybersphere is depicted as a naturally hostile landscape that women should either avoid or take special precautions before venturing into.

The notion that online aggression is simply a natural and inevitable part of the cyberscape – something David Attenborough might discuss from a safe distance in a wildlife documentary – is wrong and dangerous in its own way. Harmful agents online *are* agents, not neutral causal forces. Regardless of the esteem with which they might hold themselves, e-bilers are not forces of nature, but human beings who are responsible for their choices and who should be held accountable for their actions. Framing them as being on par with non-partisan, naturally-occurring risks such as sub-zero temperatures or seismicity gives them an extraordinary free pass to act with impunity. Further, it implies that online risk is an equal opportunity risk whereas, to cite Lindy West (2013b), 'It is not some mysterious, ambient inevitability that affects all internet users indiscriminately ... [It] is a force with a political agenda'.

On those occasions when men who attack women online are recognised *as* men (that is, as beings with agency and perhaps even some other human components) their apologists find alternative ways to exculpate them. A common tactic is to point to motivation; to claim that hostile or threatening material online should not be taken seriously or literally because its authors are intending to be funny and the targets are simply missing the joke. Facebook's 2011 response to campaigns against the proliferation of pages promoting rape and violence against women on its platform is revealing in this respect. One of these pages was called, 'You know she's playing hard to get when your chasing her down an alleyway', and had accumulated 194,370 likes on the site when rape survivors and support groups began campaigning to have it removed (Knowles, 2011). Despite the public outcry, Facebook's initial response was to refuse, arguing that the content was equivalent to *risqué* joking at a public bar: 'It is very important to point out that what one person finds offensive another can find entertaining. Just as telling a rude joke won't get you thrown out of your local pub, it won't get you thrown off Facebook' (cited in Knowles, 2011). Cath Elliott's (2011) observation at the time was that while telling rude jokes probably wouldn't result in eviction from a pub, 'propping up your local bar while inciting others to rape your mate's girlfriend "to see if she can put up a fight" would not only get you thrown out, it would in all likelihood get you arrested'.

The 'lighten up, it's just a joke' line is also well rehearsed by cyber-hate producers themselves. The alleged instigator of the campaign against Kathy Sierra, for instance, mocked her reaction as an 'insane vic-timization monologue' and dismissed his critics as having a 'psychotic censorship agenda' (Auernheimer, 2013). This man's contention was that – far from being angry or hateful – he was actually a 'prankster' engaged in a 'comedy act' (Auernheimer, 2013). Similar claims were made by Peter Nunn, the 33-year-old father brought before a court for launching a cyberhate campaign against the UK politician Stella Creasy during the debate over Criado-Perez's bank note activism (Carter, 2014). Nunn's defence in court was that he'd sent the messages to exercise his right to freedom of speech and to 'satirise' the issue of online trolling (cited in Carter, 2014). Just for the record, this alleged satire included calling Creasy an 'evil witch', then posting tweets which read, 'Best way to rape a witch, try and drown her first then just when she's gagging for air that's when you enter', and 'If you can't threaten to rape a celeb-rity, what is the point in having them?' (cited in 'Man found guilty of sending menacing tweets to Labour MP Stella Creasy', 2014). Despite his claim to clownship status, Nunn was eventually found guilty of sending indecent, obscene or menacing messages and sentenced to non-satirical jail for 18 weeks (Carter, 2014).

The 'just joking' defence of male cyberhaters is not usually accompanied by lengthy reasoning when mounted outside of academic contexts. There is, however, a substantial body of scholarly work which draws attention to the motivations of the authors of putatively hostile discourse online, often in order to prosecute the claim that outsiders (especially alarmist outsiders in the grip of moral techno-panics) are misreading and misconstruing these texts. While academic approaches will be discussed in detail in the next chapter, I note here a longstanding tendency for some researchers to privilege the motivations of authors of online hostility at the expense of tar-gets. In an influential journal article claiming to offer a precise conceptual and operational definition of flaming, Patrick B. O'Sullivan and Andrew J. Flanagin (2003) argue that authorial intention is key when diagnosing whether or not a flame is really a flame. Their case is that a flame can only be a 'true' flame if the sender's intent is to violate norms *and* both the receiver and a third-party observer agree that the communication is a violation (2003: 82).

O'Sullivan and Flanagin have received deserved praise and recognition for their painstaking efforts to acknowledge the richness of online communications. In fact, their work responds to exactly the sorts of contextual and relational nuances in communication that would be unlikely to be picked up by the Natural Language Processing Algorithm mentioned in Chapter 1. Yet their contention that a flame is not a 'true' flame unless a sender's intent is to violate norms is at odds with much of reception theory. In addition to the points raised in the previous chapter about the 'real' force of 'fake' violations, here it is also useful to consider what William K. Wimsatt Jr. and Monroe C. Beardsley (1946) call 'the intentional fallacy'. This concept supports the argument that it is neither useful nor epistemically feasible to rely on 'the design or intention' (1946: 469) of an author as a standard for arbitrating the meaning of and judging a given text. On poetry, for instance, Wimsatt and Beardsley argue that poems belong to the public and, as such, are owned neither by the critic nor the author, indeed a poem is detached from the latter 'at birth' and goes about the world beyond the poet's 'power to intend about it or control it' (1946: 470).

Returning to the intentionalist orientations of O'Sullivan and Flanagin, it seems remarkable to suggest that a self-interested party should be permitted to exercise veto power over the designation of texts which may cause harm and be in breach of various laws. Yet by these researchers' reckoning, it would not matter if a woman felt upset or frightened after receiving a message threatening rape with a combat knife. If the author of this message maintains he was simply clowning around, then the communication cannot be classified as a 'true' flame. O'Sullivan and Flanagin's insistence on the warrant of witnesses is also surprising. When applied to the discourse of sexual violence, it is uncomfortably reminiscent of those aspects of Pakistan's Law of Evidence which – prior to its overhaul in 2006 – required the 'equivalent' of four male witnesses (the testimony of two women being admissible only as one reliable source) to verify a woman's claim to having been raped (Imran, 2005: 88). A less incendiary parallel would be declaring that the necessary and sufficient conditions for determining the 'true' meaning of Shakespeare's *The Tragedy of Hamlet, Prince of Denmark* are the agreement of the author, the reader, and an impartial third party. Apart from the epistemic and conceptual problems of such a formulation, the logistical hurdles presented to English students around the globe would be most unfortunate.

The truth is that cyberhaters' motivations are radically unknowable. We could ask them about their intentions, but first we'd have to find them. And even if they were available and willing to be interviewed, how much credibility should we give to their accounts of their motivations? What if they are lying? What if they themselves are unsure of or unable to consciously access their motivations? Given the complexity of the inner world of the human, a man who uses social media to threaten a woman may not necessarily have encyclopedic insight into the entirety of his own intentions. On one hand, he may claim or genuinely believe he is sending such material not because he genuinely wishes the woman harm but because he is bored, because other people are doing it, because he thinks this is an acceptable way to express disagreement, because he wants to devise something more creative and shocking than his friends, and so on. Yet other motivations – including the intent to cause harm and the gaining of pleasure at someone else's suffering – may well be at play. In two studies published in 2014, Canadian researchers gave personality tests to 1215 subjects alongside a survey about their online commenting behaviour. They found a moderate relationship between trolling[1] and sadism, in that, 'Both trolls and sadists feel sadistic glee at the distress of others' (Buckels et al., 2014: 101). Cyber trolling, the researchers conclude, appears to be an online manifestation of 'everyday sadism' (2014: 97).

While wary of succumbing to the intentional fallacy, my conclusions are that the motivations of gendered cyberhaters are multiple, complex, and variable depending on the context. A significant number of case studies involve sole operators who seem primarily driven by personal malice against an individual woman, and who deliberately use the internet and social media platforms to stalk, harass, and threaten. Examples include those seeking to humiliate, inflict suffering on, or otherwise punish their ex-partners, as well as men who become obsessively fixated on women they have not met but who have online profiles. Many of the women

I have interviewed have been cyberstalked and harassed by both fans and antifans – the latter including men who started out as fans but who became antifans once their requests for nude photos and/or their sending of unsolicited penis pictures were ignored or rebuffed.

A different – and I suspect much larger – category of cyberhate producers *do* seem to be motivated by a desire to be funny. The intended audience for their supposedly comic material is usually made up of peers and often comes at the expense of female targets. Indeed, as per the 'gamification' of abuse discussed in Chapter 1, causing upset to the butt of a joke is an essential part of the sport. But just because a rape threat author claims they're only out for some laughs does not render their communications either funny or innocuous. As I have argued elsewhere, there is no evidence to support the idea that a flamer's self-diagnosis of 'joker' or 'prankster' exempts their target from fear, distress, or offence (Jane, 2015). Hollywood is hardly an expression of a rigorous cultural science, but it does offer an abundance of evidence that laughter is just as much the expression of the self-congratulatory scoundrel as it is the harmless and hapless jokester.

Trolls and feeding

To conclude, I will briefly address the standard advice offered to those who are abused online, which is 'don't feed the trolls'. These words of non-wisdom perfectly encapsulate the 'blame the targets/exculpate the perpetrators' dynamic described throughout this chapter. 'Don't feed the trolls' is rooted in the idea that people only attack others online in order to achieve a reaction, therefore providing no reaction will deprive them of their *raison d'être* and – magically as if by magic! – the assaults will cease. The idea is that ignoring online attackers will starve them into inaction and possibly even extinction. Whitney Phillips' observation is that, in online circles, 'don't feed the trolls' is offered as both response to and apology for all kinds of online antagonism:

> Under this logic, trolls are like great white sharks and their target's reactions like chum: the more you throw, the more worked up the shark will get (and the more likely it is that other sharks will smell the blood in the water and come join the party). Stop throwing chum, and eventually the shark will lose interest and leave. (2013)

(Note yet another framing[2] of online attackers not as human agents, but as naturally-occurring predators driven by blind instinct and animalian bloodlust rather than free will.)

The rationale behind 'don't feed the trolls' is reminiscent of the tip given to the parents of tantrum-throwing toddlers: ignore screaming children because offering either positive or negative attention will only encourage more of the unwanted behaviour. In this figuring, online attackers are infantilised. They are framed as par-formed beings whose limited or non-existent capacity for self-regulation means they cannot be held responsible for their actions like an adult (say, for example, a female adult who knows *exactly* what sort of garbage bin/snow storm/shark feeding frenzy she is exposing herself to when she blatantly chooses to connect her computer to the internet).

The 'don't feed the trolls' advice is problematic for a multitude of reasons, but here are four of them. Firstly, it doesn't work. I, for example, did not respond to a single rapey email from 1998 to 2012, yet such missives continued to arrive with monotonous regularity. The women I have interviewed report receiving a similarly constant stream of abuse regardless of whether they engage or ignore. Secondly, 'feeding' in this context often refers to talking *about* as well as talking *to* trolls. As discussed in Chapter 3, insisting that women stay silent about receiving gendered cyberhate conceals the problem. Thirdly, 'don't feed the trolls' is often used in a circular fashion to blame targets ('you asked for trolling because you fed the trolls') while also putting the onus on targets to solve the problem ('trolling will end when you stop all the troll feeding'). Fourthly, yet again this framing is exquisitely favourable to male antagonists who are relieved of all responsibility for their actions and are free to carry on with impunity.

Imagine a shopkeeper robbed at knifepoint being told to stay forever silent about the crime in the hope it stops further attacks. Or an investment fund manager chastised for reporting an embezzling employee because this will encourage more white collar crime. Aside from the special case of sexual violence against women, it is difficult to imagine any other legal context where the equivalent of 'don't feed the trolls' – that is, 'don't do anything which involves further engagement with or brings attention to the perpetrator and don't ever speak of what happened' – would be regarded as a reasonable response. I'm certain I speak for many other

Orwellian princesses when I say it is time for these unjust orientations to end. Unfortunately, 'don't feed the trolls' is not only the advice women receive informally. As the next chapter shows, it also aptly captures the response/lack-of-response of many of the powers-that-be.

Notes

1   These researchers defined 'trolling' as 'behaving in a deceptive, destructive, or disruptive manner in a social setting on the internet with no apparent instrumental purpose' (Buckels et al., 2014: 97).
2   This is a framing Phillips observes, not one she subscribes to herself (2013).

5

EPIC INSTITUTIONAL FAILS

This chapter demonstrates the way institutions have epically failed (to put it colloquially) to adequately respond to gendered cyberhate. Shortfalls that are not so epic will also be examined. In this chapter, I use the term 'institutions' loosely, and will be focusing on police, policy-makers, platform operators and corporations (including what I will call the 'gamer-industrial complex'), as well as scholars from various disciplines. It is not my intention to suggest that all representatives from all these institutions always fail female cyberhate targets all the time. I will, however, be arguing that, for the most part, institutions have done little to support women, to bring offenders to account, or to even acknowledge the problem of gendered cyberhate *as* a problem. In fact, representatives from some institutions have sometimes made things worse for female targets.

'What is Twitter?' - gendered cyberhate and police

Cyber violence against women – like violence against women of the non-cyber variety – is profoundly underreported ('Cyber violence against women and girls', 2015: 41, 2). Those targets who *do* go to police rarely receive a satisfactory response. Kathy Sierra's (2014) observation is that targets of online harassment are more likely to win the lottery than to get US law enforcement agencies to take action. Amanda Hess rang 911 after discovering a Twitter account called 'headlessfemalepig' which appeared to have been established for the sole purpose of making death threats against her (Hess, 2014). Tweets from headlessfemalepig included:

I am 36 years old, I did 12 years for 'manslaughter', I killed a woman, like you, who decided to make fun of guys cocks;

Happy to say we live in the same state. Im looking you up, and when I find you, im going to rape you and remove your head; and

You are going to die and I am the one who is going to kill you. I promise you this. (cited in Hess, 2014)

When a police officer finally arrived and a shaken Hess explained what had happened, she recalls this officer anchoring his hands on his belt, looking her directly in the eye, and asking, 'What is Twitter?' (Hess, 2014).

Other women report similarly unhelpful reactions. Jessica Valenti dealt with her first wave of rape and death threats by leaving her apartment, changing her bank accounts, and getting a new mobile phone number (Hess, 2014). When the next wave of hate crashed, she reported the abuse to law enforcement officials. The Federal Bureau of Investigation's inspired advice was to suggest she leave home until the threats blew over, to never walk outside of her apartment alone, and to be alert about any cars or men who might show up repeatedly outside her door. As Valenti puts it: 'It was totally impossible advice ... You can't just not be in a public place' (cited in Hess, 2014).

The *Time* journalist Catherine Mayer also struggled with police igno-rance when she became one of at least eight women to receive bomb threats during Caroline Criado-Perez's bank note campaign. Mayer went to London police after receiving a tweet which read: 'A BOMB HAS BEEN PLACED OUTSIDE YOUR HOME. IT WILL GO OFF AT EXACTLY 10:47PM ON A TIMER AND TRIGGER DESTROYING EVERYTHING' (cited in Mayer, 2013). None of the officers Mayer encountered used Twitter or understood why anyone would *want* to use Twitter. For Mayer, this demonstrated an abject failure to understand that, for journalists, Twitter 'ranks with the telephone and email as an essential tool of the trade' (2013). Some offic-ers thought usernames were secret codes and did not seem to understand the concept of IP addresses. They thought the best solution was for Mayer to unplug and avoid the whole cyberweb IP secret code-name spy thing altogether.

Women caught up in the GamerGate carnage have also been frustrated by their dealings with law enforcement. In 2015, Brianna Wu told *Boston*

Magazine she was losing at least a day each week 'explaining the Internet' to police (cited in Jason, 2015), in an attempt to have them understand that Twitter was not just for jokes but her primary means of marketing her business. In 2015, Wu told a journalist that she had hired a full-time staffer whose sole job was to monitor her email and Twitter mentions for death threats and hate speech (Sabin, 2015). Yet despite filing between 10 to 40 reports per day with Twitter for 'severe harassment' (Wu cited in Sabin, 2015), and making multiple reports to local law enforcement, the FBI, and Homeland Security, she says she has yet to receive a satisfactory response (O'Brien, 2015). In fact, in 2015, she felt it necessary to withdraw Giant Spacekat from the three-day PAX East gaming convention in Boston because of safety concerns for her five female employees (Borchers and Keohane, 2015). According to Wu, police had refused to increase security, even though she'd shown them the death threats she'd received via email and social media (cited in Jason, 2015).

Kath Read, meanwhile, still marvels at what happened when she informed police that her online abusers had discovered where she lived and had left the 'Hi fat bitch' note in her letterbox:

> 'Get offline and stop being so confident' was one copper's words … He was totally genuine … I don't think he was trying to be mean or anything, he just thought … 'You're doing something that's bothering people, so stop doing that thing' … It's always our fault … People aren't always malicious or mean or even judge-y about it. It's just, 'you want the problem to stop, here's the easiest way to make it stop'. (K. Read, personal communication, 2 June 2015)

Given that police forces tend to be bastions of male domination (see 'AFP staff statistics'; Crooke, 2013; 'Police workforce, England and Wales', 2015), male officers may struggle to understand women's perspectives. Indeed, on occasion police have been exposed as perpetrators of exactly the sorts of discourse women find so objectionable. In Australia in 2016, a sergeant was suspended and a Police Integrity Commission investigation launched following a media *exposé* of what was alleged to be a culture of online abuse within the force, including racism, homophobia, and comments that objectified and sexually degraded women (Duff, 2016). Among other contraventions, the suspended officer had changed his Facebook profile picture to an image of the Australian politician Jenny Leong and written, 'Nawww tank you hunny, 2 dollar sucky sucky lub you long time' (cited in Duff, 2016). Another officer, from the same inner city station, re-posted the photo of Leong with the text: 'One condom could have prevented this from happening' (cited in Duff, 2016). This was 'liked' by a number of other officers, including a senior manager. Officers revelled in the harassment of Leong, with one posting, 'She is still copping a smashing – love it!' (cited in Duff, 2016).

These anecdotal accounts of police ignorance, insensitivity, and inaction are supported by empirical data. In 74 per cent of Web Index[1] countries (including many high-income nations), law enforcement agencies and the courts are failing to take appropriate action in response to acts of gender-based violence online, while one in five female internet users live in countries where harassment and abuse of women online is extremely unlikely to be punished ('Web Index: Report 2014–15', n.d.: 15, 4). Further, approximately three-quarters of the women polled by the UK organisation Women's Aid were concerned that police were unaware of how to respond to online harassment from a partner, while 12 per cent said they had not been helped after seeking assistance (Smith, 2014).

The problem extends beyond poor attitudes and/or a lack of education among police. Consider Jane – the nurse whose former boyfriend's posting of a naked photo of her on a revenge porn site along with her contact details led to anonymous calls and emails (Citron and Franks, 2014: 101). Police told Jane they could not act because her ex-boyfriend had not engaged in ongoing harassment – that is, he'd posted only a single photo, and had not explicitly solicited others to stalk her (Citron, 2014b). The gross inadequacy of this reaction highlights the manifest deficiencies of the legislation underlying police responses. In the UK, the chief constable responsible for fighting digital crime, Stephen Kavanagh, admits that the 'unimagined scale of online abuse' threatens to overwhelm the police service (cited in Laville, 2016). Noting that existing laws include one dating back to the 19th century, he has called for new and more simplified legislation in the hope of achieving justice for tens of thousands of targets (Laville, 2016).

While all this paints a grim picture, there have been a handful of arrests in relation to the abuse and harassment of women and girls online. The sextortionist Luis Mijangos, for instance, pled guilty to one count of computer hacking and one count of wiretapping and was sentenced to six years imprisonment (Wittes et al., 2016). In the UK in January 2014, a woman and a man were jailed for 12 weeks and eight weeks respectively, for abusive and threatening tweets sent to Caroline Criado-Perez (Cockerell, 2014). Two years later, in Germany, a court ruled that a Facebook user would face a fine of up to 250,000 euros if they did not cease posting racist, misogynistic, and harassing comments to the page of the female journalist Dunja Hayali (Dillon, 2016). In Australia in two separate cases in 2016, two men who had abused women over Facebook each pled guilty to the charge of 'using a carriage service to menace, harass or cause offence', which carries a maximum jail sentence of three years (Taylor, 2016; Vernon, 2016). One was sentenced to an eight-month suspended jail sentence, and the other was sentenced to a 12-month good behaviour bond."

'A mad fucking witch' – gendered cyberhate and policy-makers

Given this book's broad focus, it might seem foolish to generalise about the state of 'the law' given the countless variations in legislation in different nations and jurisdictions. Yet a 2014 report by the Association for Progressive Communications (APC) identifies multiple policy failures at an international level in this regard. Despite an increase in violence against women involving information and communications technology (ICT), the APC finds 'very little corresponding recognition of ICT-related forms of violence against women by states, intergovernmental institutions and other actors responsible for ending violence against women' ('Domestic legal remedies for technology-related violence against women: Review of related studies and literature', 2014: 4). The existence of outdated legislation is problematic in that it can be difficult to apply 'existing norms to a technology that did not exist at the time the laws were drafted' (2014: 15). Yet the APC points out that ICT-related violence against women is not being prioritised: in prevention and response strategies; in budgeting; or in evidence-based policy-making (2014: 4). This leaves women who experience these violations with little or no redress (2014: 4). (Readers interested in greater detail and individual case studies can look to the work of Citron, who provides extensive coverage – albeit mostly from a US perspective – of various failures to apply existing laws to cyber harassment (see Citron, 2014a, 2014b, 2014c; and Citron and Franks, 2014).)

A frequent observation made by women targeted for misogyny online is that, like police, many policy-makers seem to lack awareness about the full extent and seriousness of the problem, and appear to hold the belief that opting out of the cybersphere is a viable solution. Echoing issues raised in Chapter 4, Kath Read thinks many politicians view the internet as being like a Gameboy – a pleasant enough diversion, but something women can easily live without. The wrong-headedness of such views may be related to the age of many elected representatives. Figures from 2013, for instance, show that the average politician in the US, UK, Canada, and Australia was 50 or older ('The 43rd Parliament: Traits and trends', 2013). This means most policy-makers are not digital natives – that is, they came late to the internet and social media rather than growing up with these systems and platforms as an integrated part of contemporary life. That 78 per cent of the world's national parliamentarians are men ('Facts and figures: Leadership and political participation', 2016) may also mean they struggle to appreciate how it feels to be bombarded by threats containing explicit imagery about, say, the vaginal damage that will be caused by a gang rape involving sharp objects.

As with the 'sucky sucky' case study described above (Duff, 2016), it is telling that male politicians are sometimes caught circulating similarly offensive material themselves. 'Sexting' scandals, such as those involving the former US Congressman Anthony Weiner and the Indiana Democrat Justin Moed (Chasmar, 2015), suggest at least some male politicians lack awareness about the inappropriateness of, for example, sending women unsolicited 'dick pics'. In Australia in 2015, meanwhile, the former federal Labor leader Mark Latham was exposed as the man behind a Twitter account which had been engaged in the sustained trolling of a number of prominent feminists and journalists (Noyes, 2015). The following year, that nation's federal immigration minister was outed as having described – via text message – a senior political journalist who had exposed a sexual harassment incident at a high level in Australian politics as 'a mad fucking witch' (Medhora, 2016). That male political representatives make such comments and engage in such behaviour gives women good reason to be pessimistic about their capacity to recognise gendered cyberhate as a problem and take action.

One politician who does know what it's like to be on the other end of sexist cyber abuse is Nicole Lawder,[2] a member of the Australian Capital Territory Legislative Assembly. During campaigning for a 2012 election, Lawder's appearance was pilloried online because a throat tumour was causing a visible lump in her neck under her chin:

It was a benign tumour, it wasn't doing anyone any harm, but it ... made my neck look fatter than it really needed to. I often sat with my hand over my chin so people couldn't see it, then [a web site devoted to Australian politics] specifically focused on my fat neck. After that I felt so ... demoralised, I ... had it removed ... At that time I was maybe 50, I'd been the CEO of two different national organisations and you would have hoped that people might judge you on what you stood for and what your values were rather than how you looked. (N. Lawder, personal communication, 7 July 2015)

When policy-makers do not recognise or adequately respond to the harm of gendered cyberhate, they are failing to follow through on the commitment by an increasing number of nations to address internet-related equity issues in recognition of the vital economic and social role played by affordable and effective broadband. For instance, by mid-2015, a full 148 countries had a national broadband plan or strategy in place ('The state of broadband 2015', 2015: 10). The UN Broadband Commission has acknowledged, however, that various digital divides are proving 'stubbornly persistent', with the gender digital divide especially difficult to overcome (2015: 8–9). In particular, it says access to technology needs to be combined with the 'relevant skills, opportunities and capabilities', and that this is another divide that is especially visible in terms of its gendered dimension (2015: 9–10)

'Opportunities' is a key term, here, because – as discussed in Chapter 3– the proliferation of gendered cyberhate is reducing the ways women are able to participate and engage on the internet. Equity online involves not only equal access in terms of computer hardware and network connections, but equality in terms of how various platforms can be used. A woman may have a perfectly functional laptop with the latest operating system and access to affordable, high-speed broadband, yet still have her online options severely constricted in terms of where she feels able to go, and what she feels able to say. Female targets of cyberhate are being disenfranchised when they are harassed and pushed out of online fora that would otherwise allow them safe participation in digital citizenship and the digital economy. As such, a policy focus only on access to hardware and fast broadband can give rise to the illusion of full participation, and the masking of powerlessness and oppression.

The spike in international concern about gendered cyberhate – especially since GamerGate – does mean a number of countries are currently reviewing existing laws and/or drafting new ones. Legislation relating to revenge porn now exists in the UK, the Philippines, Israel, Canada, and Japan, as well as in some states in the US and Australia (Henry, 2015). Further, more policy-makers are showing awareness of the problem and are agitating for action. In the US in 2015, for instance, Congresswoman Katherine Clark (2015) noted that federal prosecutors had pursued only 10 of the estimated 2.5 million cases of cyberstalking between 2010 and 2013, even though it is a federal crime in that nation. She called on the Department of Justice to lift its game by investigating and prosecuting more cases involving online threats to rape and murder women. Indeed, Clark revealed that she had had first-hand experience of online harassment, and that even *she* had been told by the authorities to just ignore it: 'There's not an understanding yet of how quick and powerful the Internet can be for destructive purposes. We shouldn't have to wait for the case where someone is killed' (cited in Jason, 2015).

'We suck at dealing with abuse and ... we've sucked at it for years' – gendered cyberhate and corporations

As with the failures in relation to police and policy-makers identified above, the inaction and unhelpfulness of social media platforms such as Facebook and Twitter are a recurring theme in the accounts given by female targets of cyberhate. Again, individual circumstances vary, and platforms are constantly changing their interfaces and reporting functions. In general, however, women's criticisms are that reporting abuse is: (a) prohibitively time consuming; and (b) unlikely to result in any sort of meaningful assistance. Further, attackers who are blocked or suspended are notorious for simply making new accounts and starting the cyberhate 'rinse and repeat' cycle all over again.

The seemingly arbitrary nature of some of the decisions made by social media platforms and other 'corporate bystanders' (Powell and Henry, 2015b) is a source of immense frustration. Clementine Ford – perhaps Australia's most cyberhated feminist – has twice been banned from her own Facebook page because the social media giant decided she had violated its 'community standards' in her attempts to deal with male abusers. On the first occasion, in 2015, Ford was banned for re-publishing screenshots of the abuse men had sent her. As she put it in a series of tweets at the time:

It's fine for men to message you to call you a filthy whore but it's breaching 'community standards' to post it for people to see ... Women are subjected to heinous abuse online and they're the ones punished for speaking out about it? ... We have to keep quiet about it and 'protect the privacy' of men who send unsolicited photos of their dicks and call you a whore. (cited in Sainty, 2015)

Complaints about Twitter are also numerous. In 2016, a parody Twitter account was established to mock the platform's 'terribly inconsistent' enforcement of harassment policies, which, it was said, too often punished and suspended 'all the wrong people while at the same time allowing known harassers to run rampant throughout their system' (Lachenal, 2016). Tweets posted by the @trustysupport account included:

> Some users are currently experiencing harassment and abuse on @Twitter. We are aware of the issue and are not working towards a resolution.

> Are you a white male harasser? @Twitter is here for you. Click the new 'Help, My Free Speech!' button for instant @Support #TwitterTips.

And:

> Today @Twitter would like to announce our new Harassment Policy: Every new user will receive FREE ABUSE with their new Twitter account. ('Trusty Support')

Twitter's response to this attempt to draw attention to its inconsistent, ineffective, and incoherent responses to harassment was to temporarily suspend the parody account – a move a journalist dubbed 'meta-satire' (Jeong, 2016). The comedian Amy Schumer was similarly mocking in a sketch involving the introduction of a social media 'I'm going to rape and kill you' button designed to save attackers valuable time and character space (Flynn, 2016).

Yet again, anecdotal accounts of inadequate or non-existent platform responses to gendered cyberhate are backed up by data from the APC. Its report on violence against women online compares the policies of Facebook, YouTube, and Twitter, and identifies a number of overarching problems including:

- a reluctance to engage directly with technology-related violence against women, until it becomes a public relations issue;
- a lack of transparency around reporting and redress processes;
- a failure to engage with the perspectives of non-North American/ European women; and
- no public commitment to human rights standards or to the promotion of rights, other than the encouragement of free speech. (Nyst, 2014: 3–4)

For the APC, these failings suggest a lack of appreciation of the seriousness of violence against women online, as well as a lack of recognition of the responsibility of platforms to intervene (Nyst, 2014). Behind closed doors, however, at least one captain of techno industry has been more forthcoming with a *mea culpa*. In a memo leaked to the media in 2015, Twitter CEO Dick Costolo was caught out admitting to employees that:

> We suck at dealing with abuse and trolls on the platform and we've sucked at it for years. It's no secret and the rest of the world talks about it every day. We lose core user after core user by not addressing simple trolling issues that they face every day. I'm frankly ashamed of how poorly we've dealt with this issue during my tenure as CEO. (cited in Tiku and Newton, 2015)

'Nothing ruins a good party like uncomfortable guests'

Also sucking at dealing with abuse are the video game corporations, organisations, groups, and consumers that together make up the gamer-industrial complex. Poor attitudes towards women are deeply entrenched in the corporate institutions associated with gamer fan cultures. Thus the sexism in games-related corporations and products, and games-related fan cultures are likely co-constitutive.

While most criticism of the tech and gaming industries has been generated by outsiders looking in, a notable exception came in 2007 when Aaron Swartz, a much-admired programmer and 'hacktivist', issued a stinging attack on the tech community's mistreatment of women (cited in Lenssen, 2007). Swartz drew attention to a sexist work culture that manifested in, among other objectionable practices, industry elites routinely holding key business meetings in strip clubs:

> If you talk to any woman in the tech community, it won't be long before they start telling you stories about disgusting, sexist things guys have said to them. It freaks them out; and rightly so. As a result, the only women you see in tech are those who are willing to put up with all the abuse ... The denial about this in the tech community is so great that sometimes I despair of it ever getting fixed. (Swartz cited in Lenssen, 2007)

A recent case concerns the 'star' software engineer Jessie Frazelle, who was one of the main coders for the start-up Docker before she left the company, apparently for harassment-related reasons (Bort, 2016). In a post headlined

'This industry is fucked', Frazelle describes the endless harassment she has experienced since beginning to speak regularly at conferences and to contribute to open source projects (that is, since becoming successful in her chosen career):

> I've gotten hundreds of private messages on IRC and emails about sex, rape, and death threats. People emailing me saying they jerked off to my conference talk video (you're welcome btw) is mild in comparison to sending photoshopped pictures of me covered in blood. I wish I could do my job, something I very obviously love doing, without any of this bullshit. However that seems impossible at this point. (Bort, 2015)

Given such observations, it is not surprising that the number of women working in tech is small and getting smaller. While 35 per cent of computing jobs in the US were held by women in 1990 (Corbett and Hill, 2015: 9), this had fallen to 25 per cent by 2015 ('By the numbers', 2016). Further, 76 per cent of games developers are men (Gaudiosi, 2014) even though, as previously discussed, nearly half their US customers are women (Duggan, 2015).

The predominance of male game designers may help explain why – as Anita Sarkeesian tirelessly points out – many popular video games continue to reinforce oppressive gender stereotypes via tropes such as women as background decoration, women as damsels in distress, and women as prizes. Examples of the latter include players having sex with female sex workers as a means of unlocking rewards and boosting in-game abilities. Players are also rewarded for finding and collecting images of nude women, and for 'in-game behaviour that amounts to sexual harassment' (Sarkeesian, 2015b). Angry backlashes have occurred when straight male players encounter games that are not made 'exclusively with their fantasies in mind' (Sarkeesian, 2015b). Examples include role-playing games in which they must interact with gay male characters, or lesbian characters unavailable as romance options to male avatars. Furious protests from straight male players have also ensued when Western releases of Japanese games 'place women in slightly less revealing outfits, or increase the age of young sexualised female characters to 18' (Sarkeesian, 2015b).

A chicken-and-the-egg question arises around which came first (or at least which represents the most powerful driving force): top-down sexism from games companies or bottom-up demand from game players. Media effects are complex and contested, and it would be laughable to suggest that men are abusing women online because sexist video game content is somehow controlling their behaviour. That said, it would be equally ridiculous to contend that sexist tropes games have no relationship at all with the longstanding and structural 'misogyny and violence' evident in hypermasculine games communities (Jenson and de Castell, 2013: 74–5, 80). A mid-ground position that bypasses the 'monkey see, monkey do' version of media effects is to see male consumer demand and video game supply as existing in a feedback loop in which the preferences of the former and the content of the latter constitute and reinforce each other. The net result is the continued production of many popular games which are hostile to – or oppressive and demeaning for – women, even as the latter make up a larger and larger customer base. As such, Sarkeesian's argument that in-game cultures of objectification of and male entitlement to women are likely to percolate into the broader culture is persuasive.

The interrelation between gamer-related corporations and fan cultures is also evident in the way GamerGaters continue to operate as a powerful – albeit chaotic – lobby group. In 2015, the high-profile digital culture summit South by Southwest (SXSW) made the decision to cancel a proposed 2016 panel on overcoming harassment in games in response to threats of harassment, apparently from GamerGaters (Alexander, 2015). In the face of a media backlash in response to the cancellation, SXSW director Hugh Forrest admitted the festival had made a mistake and announced that a day-long summit on the topic of online harassment would be staged during the 2016 event. In a piece critical of the initial SXSW 'debacle', the tech journalist Leigh Alexander (2015) slams not only the below-the-belt harassment campaigns of GamerGaters but the consequent acquiescence of the powers-that-be. She recalls, for instance, that when she wrote an editorial critical of sexism in video game culture, GamerGaters responded by 'swarming Intel with "consumer complaints" until it pulled advertisements' from the site that had published her piece (2015).

Reminiscent of the GTFO approach to gender was one gamer-related group's bright idea to remedy digital misogyny by removing women from the equation entirely. In 2011, the Texan organisers of a large local-area network (LAN) gathering scheduled to celebrate the launch of a military-style, first-person shooter game decided the best way to ensure no female gamers were harassed was to ensure no female gamers were allowed to attend. In the original FAQ section for the event, the organisers wrote that:

> Nothing ruins a good LAN party like uncomfortable guests or lots of tension, both of which can result from mixing immature, misogynistic male-gamers with female counterparts. Though we've done our best to avoid these situations in years past, we've certainly had our share of problems. As a result, we no longer allow women to attend this event. (cited in Good, 2011)

The language is politer than 'GTFO', but the net result is the same: women are excluded and punished (if being prevented from attending such an event with such people is indeed a punishment), while 'immature, misogynistic male-gamers' are given a free ride. Once again, the subtext is that men could not possibly possess the agency required to regulate or be held responsible for their actions, so all interventions focus on the women. It's yet another men-as-forces-of-nature framing in which destruction can be anticipated and maybe mitigated via prophylaxis but never controlled.

'Perhaps the reason why so much flaming is not taken seriously is due to its spelling and grammatical errors' – gendered cyberhate and scholarship

The final section of this chapter extends Chapter 4's critique of trends in some scholarly coverage of hostility online. The material in this section is a precis of a 20,000-word paper called 'Flaming? What flaming? The pitfalls and potentials of researching online hostility', published in the journal *Ethics and Information Technology* (Jane, 2015). I mention this: (1) to direct readers' attention to the detailed interdisciplinary literature review underpinning this section; (2) to acknowledge that the broad claims I am about to make are necessarily missing fine detail and nuance; and (3) to apologise for the fact that, by citing here only a few of the scholars whose work is discussed in my original article, I might give the impression that they are being singled out for special attention. I regret the latter but am concerned that citing *no* examples of the academic orientations to which I am drawing attention would greatly weaken my case.

Patterns in academia may be of only passing interest to those outside scholarship, and studying these might appear to be indulgent, ivory tower naval gazing. Yet while it would be hubristic to inflate the importance of a job I myself happen to hold, scholarly research does have the potential to influence policy, as well as to provide powerful support for those advocating for social change. I therefore find myself aligned – if only in principle – with GamerGaters in believing that the way academics conduct research *matters*, and, as such, deserves close examination. Further, while police, governments, and corporations, are being intensely scrutinised for their actions and inactions in relation to online hostility, academics researching the topic have not been subjected to the same level – or indeed much of any type – of interrogation. Thus this section is designed to fill a niche but nevertheless important gap. That academics are being closely monitored by GamerGaters (some of whom see us as part of The Enemy) is also a timely reminder for scholars that we may be part of the phenomenon we are mapping, measuring, and analysing. It increases the need for us to engage in rigorous self-reflexivity as we conduct our inquiries.

While many aspects of gendered cyberhate are new in terms of prevalence, rhetorical noxiousness, and stark misogyny, hostility has always been part of computer-mediated communication (CMC), and has been addressed by scholars from a range of disciplines and through a range of theoretical lenses since the 1980s. The *objects* of these historical analyses are – by my account – prototypes of, variations on, close relations to, and/or sub-sets of the type of cyberhate addressed in this book and help explain why contemporary misogyny online presents the way it does. By the same token, the scholarly *analyses* of these objects show that examining this discourse has presented various conceptual, methodological, and epistemological challenges. Having reviewed more than three decades of research into hostile discourse and CMC (Jane, 2015), my conclusion is that when online hostility is coded as 'trolling' or 'flaming' it has tended to be underplayed, overlooked, or otherwise marginalised. This has resulted in a somewhat skewed body of literature – though in the reverse direction than that claimed by GamerGaters.

Scholarly literature on discourse designated as 'flaming' can be arranged into three waves. The first mostly concerns debate about 'computer effects', that is, whether hostile communications are the result of computers or social contexts. Eventually, it is decided that online invective probably involves both. The second wave of research, published mostly in the early 21st century, involves increasingly meticulous attempts to characterise what can and cannot be construed as a flame (cf. Thompsen and Foulger, 1996: 228–9; O'Sullivan and Flanagin, 2003; Turnage, 2007; Kaufer, 2000: 5–14). This second wave of research – by my account – changed the framing of the debate about flaming from social, ethical, and political issues to arguments about definitions and methodology. The subsequent lack of an adequate definition of 'flaming' helps explain what is, in essence, a phantom third wave: that is, a conspicuous absence of discussions of online hostility in texts such as internet studies handbooks. For example, the topics of flaming and trolling do not appear in the 57 chapters which together make up Springer's *International Handbook of Internet Research* (Hunsinger et al., 2010), and *The Oxford Handbook of Internet Studies* (Dutton, 2013). Wiley-Blackwell's *The Handbook of Internet Studies* (Consalvo and Ess, 2011), meanwhile, makes only passing mentions of flaming and trolling over its 22 chapters.

Scholarly approaches in the three waves discussed above have commonalities as well as differences. For example, research obstacles – such as the difficulties associated with definition, reception, and the collection of reliable empirical data – are frequently 'resolved' in favour of flamers whose production of vitriol online is exculpated and sometimes celebrated (for examples of the latter see Jane, 2015: 74–76). Also common is the use of vague generalisations (such as describing flaming as 'hostile expression' (Lea et al., 1992: 89)), alongside what appears to me to be a reluctance to quote real examples of explicit vitriol, particularly in early research work. While this might be due, at least in part, to the fact that early cyberhate tended to be far milder than its current forms, I suspect there also exists a degree of academic squeamishness and lack of understanding about the colloquialisms associated with language online. Insight into scholarly thinking around the latter can be found in an anonymous reader's comment responding to a paper I submitted to a highly ranked international journal in the field. This reviewer suggested that: 'Perhaps the reason why so much flaming is not taken seriously is due to its spelling and grammatical errors; so if the flamer is a poor writer, the flames have no credibility and are ignored' (cited in Jane, 2015: 72). This orientation conflicts with digital media scholar Alfred Hermida's advice to journalists that tests to determine the credibility of social media accounts of breaking news events are often the reverse of what they would be in mainstream media contexts: 'If you see a message with swearing, with grammatical errors, chances are it's likely to be credible ... Punctuation mistakes, swearing adds to the credibility and authenticity of a message' (cited in Aedy, 2013). While Hermida's observation relates specifically to breaking news events, it does lend support to my case that a rape or death threat might still be taken seriously by a receiver even if it is missing apostrophes or capitalisations.

Further insight into academic debate around what is and is not considered offensive can be found in the work of Philip A. Thompsen and Davis A. Foulger (1996). They use the term 'profane antagonism' to describe an exchange involving the words 'damn' and 'crap', and in which a skier named 'Snow Pro' asks someone who calls themselves 'Dr. Ski' whether their diploma is 'from a cereal box?:-)' (1996: 243, emoticon in original). Thompsen and Foulger's position is that such messages are exemplars of flames at the most extreme end of the spectrum and may represent 'a state beyond antagonism' (1996: 228). While casting aspersions on the legitimacy of one's PhD qualifications may seem profane to academics, relatively speaking these messages are really quite friendly. Consider, too, the vast difference between 'I had to ask about three people to figure out how to get the @#$%*ing insertion point beyond a graphics frame' (a message coded as an uninhibited flame demonstrating 'profanity, negative affect, and typographic energy' by Lee Sproull and Sara Kiesler in an investigation into the effect of decreasing social context cues on communication; 1986: 1508), and an online discussion about the feminist Germaine Greer on the Men Are Better Than Women website. The latter refers to the feminist writer as a 'stupid cunt' and a filthy, drugged-up, well-abused whore who 'looks like a fucking beige batting glove left in the sun with a wad of stringy doll's hair stapled to the palm' (Masterson, 2006a, 2006b). It describes feminists in general as 'hags' with 'slime-infested cunt[s]' who fabricate rape allegations and whose opinions are only ever a 'cluster fuck of malformed logic'.

Further, while cyberhate has certainly become more graphic in recent years, I received the aforementioned reviewer's comment about spelling and grammatical errors in 2013. The following year I also received, in similar circumstances, feedback chastising me for citing unexpurgated examples of gendered cyberhate in academic work. I was advised that even researchers 'examining avant-garde sexual practices don't use such language' and was asked to please remove it.[3] Given that this man also questioned my overall argument on the grounds that he himself had not noticed any misogyny online, it was frustrating – and I think indicative of a larger scholarly phenomenon – that he did not wish to be exposed to the very evidence that would have supported my thesis. While an increasing number of academics are now citing unexpurgated examples of cyberhate, the two comments above do suggest that at least some might still be shying away from a close examination of such material because of squeamishness and/or because they assume its colloquialism and profanity disqualify it as a legitimate object for scholarly consideration.

Regardless of individual researchers' tastes and tolerance for material outside their comfort zones, when academics cite only the tamest examples or rely on euphemisms, they inadvertently position online hostility as a mild and mostly benign practice. Thus it becomes all too easy to overlook the real harms done to real targets in real ways, and to instead look for more positive aspects of the discourse. This helps explain the somewhat counterintuitive link between the unspeakability of the content pro-duced by flamers and trolls, and the fact that some scholars – and aspiring scholars in the form of PhD candidates – invite reconsiderations of such communications as less destructive or hostile than might have previously been assumed (see Postmes et al., 2000; McKee, 2002; Vrooman, 2002; Lee, 2005; Lange, 2006, 2007; Kuntsman, 2007; Douglas, 2008; Milne, 2010; McCosker, 2013; Manivannan, 2013). Hongjie Wang, for example, claims that flaming in an academic discussion group 'educates the ignorant', 'tames the uncouth', enforces 'netiquette', promotes 'good writing and effective communication' and 'scares away commercial advertizing' (1996). E. Gabriella Coleman, meanwhile, writes of the 'rich aesthetic tradition of spectacle and transgression' associated with the increasing number of internet dwellers who engage in 'acts of merciless mockery/flaming', 'morally dicey pranking', and 'ultra coordinated motherfuckary' (2012: 101, 110). Yet she maintains there are still forms of moral constraint at work and that – as the kind of 'trickster' posed by Lewis Hyde – trolls may be helping to renew both culture and the world by disturbing established categories of truth and property (2012: 115). In 2013, meanwhile, a spe-cial journal edition that had invited consideration of the generative rather than destructive qualities of trolling (Wilson et al., 2012) included a con-tribution arguing that the putative misogyny of 4chan contributors who call women 'cumdumpsters' needs to be appreciated not as evidence of widespread prejudice but as a strategic, regenerative practice calculated to preserve subcultural integrity (Manivannan, 2013).

Many researchers in this area make the case – either explicitly or implicitly – that reconceptualisations of online hostility are required as a sorely-needed corrective to a majoritarian view in scholarship overstating prevalence and impact. It is difficult, however, to locate this supposed technophobic orthodoxy anywhere other than in extremely early CMC-related research. Also, while some mainstream media coverage reads as simplistic and sensational scaremongering, there also exists a significant number of sober and well-reasoned media texts which provide valuable insights into the ambit, tenor, and targets of contemporary gendered cyberhate (see Jackman, 2011; Hess, 2014; Sandoval, 2013; Jason, 2015). Thus researchers who express desire to distance themselves from simplistic, technology-related 'moral panics'[4] in popular discourse (see McKenna and Bargh, 2000; Phillips, 2011; McCosker, 2013: 203) may themselves be engaged in a degree of over-simplification.

Defenses or celebrations of online vitriol are not of logical necessity inherently problematic. In many instances and from some perspectives, the production and circulation of vitriol can indeed be pleasurable, cathartic, creative, entertaining, funny, performative, subversive, educational, empowering, and part of a strategy of counterhegemonic resistance. Yet while such discourse may well assist in building relationships, staking boundaries, forging identities, facilitating group formations, and so on, the same could be said about the racist commentary circulating around white supremacist sites such as Stormfront. Further, while many academic texts on flaming make valid points when read in isolation, looking at this work as a canon suggests a narrow and even biased approach in that scholars have tended to look for optimistic readings of flaming and trolling at the expense of considering their serious ethical and material ramifications (Jane, 2015).

In recent years, these patterns in scholarship have shifted due to an upsurge of interest in misogyny online from feminist researchers, especially feminist legal scholars (see Citron, 2014a, 2014b, 2014c; Citron and Franks, 2014; Henry and Powell, 2015; Mantilla, 2015). This is extremely encouraging. Newcomers to the field should bear in mind, however, that engaging in such research can be risky if it receives the sort of media coverage academics are under increasing pressure to secure to demonstrate the impact of their work. Alison Phipps is a UK scholar whose research on 'lad cultures' and sexual violence in higher education receives much media coverage – and consequently much gendered cyberhate. Comments that have been emailed to her directly or written about her online call her a prude, an idiot, and a man-hater, describing her as joyless, vapid, toxic and entitled (Phipps, 2014). Remarks have been made about her appearance and, 'as seems to be becoming inevitable for women with opinions', specifically about her genitals (Phipps, 2014).

Having lived mostly cyberhate free from 2012 to 2014 – a period when my public profile was low – attacks on me commenced again in 2015 when I began doing media interviews about the research underpinning this book. In one YouTube clip, a critic says that, by drawing attention to the fact that women don't enjoy being threatened with death by dismemberment, I am revealing my gender's weak spots and am therefore encouraging more attacks. (While disagreeing with most of this commentator's points, I do respect his strong views on not giving individual trolls publicity, and so will refrain from providing a reference for his work.) This man – let's call him Huge Weakness Dude – uses voice-changing technology to explain that men aren't targeted for gendered insults because they are not socially conditioned to respond to gendered insults. We women, on the other hand, are 'trained to be perfect targets' by constantly telling ourselves and each other that certain words should hurt us.

In this clip, Huge Weakness Dude seems to address me directly when he critiques my misogyny-on-the-internet thesis as ludicrously hyperbolic and alarmist. After citing my work, he then says, in his computerised deadpan: 'Careful slut, them's rapin words'. This threat/'threat' is apparently being deployed ironically in that the subtext seems to be, 'this is exactly the kind of statement feminists are stupid and hugely weak enough to misinterpret and interpret as a rape threat'. There is much appreciation of the hilarity of 'Careful slut, them's rapin' words' in the comments beneath Huge Weakness Dude's clip. One contributor says – in relation to a photo shown of me – that I have 'crazy eyes', while others call me a child, ridiculously insane, a fucking hack, and 'a fucking imbecile jumping on the I'm a victim narrative'. It is claimed that the material I cite as having received myself is either fabricated or self-sent, and that I have fallen for the fabrications of Anita Sarkeesian, Brianna Wu, Zoë Quinn, and Laurie Penny who are all 'proven professional victims and liars'. Someone else calls on women to stop being 'pissy babies' or they'll rape our arses and skull fuck our dead mothers. As with Huge Weakness Dude's warning/'warning' about me being raped/'raped' if I don't shut up, the contextual implication is that these threatening insults are being offered up as exactly the sort of harmless, non-threatening, non-insults crazy-eyed feminists are misreading *as* insults – which, of course, is insult in itself. My view is that this linguistic ambivalence is being exploited by attackers, in that it permits the issuing of threats of sexual violence in a manner which contains a sort of built-in, pre-planned defence. (It is reminiscent of the headline 'Ironic porn purchase leads to unironic ejaculation' from the satirical website *The Onion* back in 1999.)

There is also a pro-GamerGate thread on Reddit suggesting 'a new op for dealing with the problem of establishment academia and its attempts to dictate media … to conform to authoritarian leftist politics' (nochafaa, 2015). I am named, alongside another of my Sydney colleagues whose gaming research is not liked by GamerGaters. Participants either imply or say outright that we are liars, 'pseudo researchers', and 'SocJus[5] trash' who are guilty of 'immoral slandering', 'mind poison', weaving a 'web of interconnecting bogus citations', and 'academic corruption' (nochafaa and comments beneath nochafaa, 2015). While there is some disagreement about tactics,[6] suggested strategies include lobbying our employers to have us disciplined for lack of academic integrity. One contributor re-posts an email already sent to 'the head' of my university aiming to achieve this objective (Gamergating commenting beneath nochafaa, 2015). As one contributor put it, 'this is the arena where Gamergate can inflict some serious damage and ruin some careers' (buck_fiddle commenting beneath nochafaa, 2015). Participants/operatives are urged to hit academics where it hurts by hunting for plagiarism in our masters and doctoral theses because, 'Group projects of [this] kind … are extremely successful, and the result … is that these people lose their academic titles' (Phrenologicus commenting beneath nochafaa, 2015). As another contributor says, 'it's ridiculously easy to derail the career of a young academic (the kind who would be doing this kind of research)' (buck_fiddle commenting beneath nochafaa, 2015).

I am relieved to report that, at the time of writing at least, I still held my academic title. That said, perhaps this is only because one contributor to this thread on the importance of accuracy seems confused about whether my name is actually 'Emma A. Jane' or 'Emma A Jones' (Gamergating commenting beneath nochafaa, 2015). In the meantime, I'm sure I'm not the only academic who would welcome the assistance of recreational plagiarism hunters during essay-marking season.

Six degrees of excuse-making

Over the course of this chapter I have illustrated the various ways institutions have failed to adequately support or assist women who are targeted for cyberhate. Rather than accusing any single authority of being more negligent than any other, I have shown the way the shortcomings of a range of institutions are integrated and feed into each other. Alongside this dearth of helpfulness, there exists a surplus of excuse-making and rationalisation. Thematically these tend to fall into one or more of the following six categories:

- *Apologies* (we're sorry; we were caught off guard; we didn't realise; we're doing our best; we're helping as fast as we can; oh, and could you please explain again how the internet...?)
- *Excuses* (there's too much of it; there's not enough of us; the old laws are too old; the new laws aren't ready; it's all too hard; it's all too expensive; it's all too anonymous; none of it is our fault; and couldn't someone else please fix it?)
- *Denial* (it's not so bad; there's not so much of it; there'll always be rude language online; men have it just as tough; it's just words; it's just the internet; there really is nothing to see here, so please move along)
- *Accusations* (you went to the wrong place; you said the wrong thing; you posted the wrong picture; you took too many risks; you must have known; you have only yourself to blame; we'd never say you were asking for it but, hey, lady, you were so totally asking for it)
- *Defense of attackers* (it's a media beat-up; it's a moral panic; trolls are funny; trolls are misunderstood; trolls are cool; trolls are ironic; trolls are doing edgy boundary work; and did we not already explain how troll misogyny ≠ *real* misogyny?)
- *Libertarianism* (free speech is good; regulation is bad; rape threats are better than censorship; intervention = totalitarianism).

While some of these excuses are understandable and/or reasonable some of the time, together they constitute an unforgivable shirking of responsibility. In its 2015 report, the UN Broadband Commission warns that cyber VAWG risks producing a 'global pandemic with significant negative consequences for all societies in general and irreparable damage for girls and women in particular' ('Cyber violence against women and girls: A world-wide wake-up call', 2015: 6–7). I agree, given the magnitude of the problem, the making of excuses must end and the taking of action must start. Platforms need to stop 'sucking' at dealing with abuse. Police need to Google 'Twitter'. Laws need to be enforced, updated, or written from scratch. And some actual perpetrators need to be brought to account.

The main argument mounted against the regulation of gendered hate speech online involves the well-worn claim that limiting *any* aspect of speech anywhere will have us all skidding down a slippery slope into nefarious censorship and Big Brother totalitarianism. This approach is not only unhelpful; it advocates an entirely unprecedented social and political arrangement. David van Mill (2015), for instance, points out that there has never existed a society in which speech has not been limited to some extent. He also rejects the proposition that we can choose to be either on or off this slippery slope. Rather, we are *necessarily* on the slope whether we like it or not: 'the task is always to decide how far up or down we choose to go, not whether we should step off the slope altogether' (2015). Free speech chicken littles should also note that the slippery-slope argument 'works' just as well for their big government nemeses: remove a single government intervention and we'll all career down the slippery slope into *Lord of the Flies*-style anarchy and savagery.

The question, therefore, changes from, 'should speech be limited?' to 'under what circumstances is limiting speech justified?'. The two most important formulations invoked to argue both for and against the use of coercive state power to stymie freedom of expression are John Stuart Mill's 'harm principle' (1863) and Joel Feinberg's 'offence principle' (1985). Both offer possibilities for thinking through broader tensions between liberty and authority in order to decide when limiting speech might be justified. The body of literature involving forensic academic analyses and interpretations of the harm and offence principles is enormous. Rather than risk exposing these to repetitive citation injury by revisiting them all again here, I will simply state my case, which is that some (though not all) gendered cyberhate can cause harm and offence of the sort which is sufficiently serious to warrant state involvement. This may include (but not necessarily be limited to) the introduction and imposing of various regulations, which may result in the punishment of offenders in forms such as fines and/or jail terms. Limitations on speech should indeed be avoided where possible, but, in the case of much gendered cyberhate, the harm of not regulating this speech is greater than the harm of allowing it to continue to circulate unobstructed.

This position follows Stanley Eugene Fish's (1994) rejection of the idea that the (inevitable) limits on speech can be determined ahead of time via abstract reasoning or general principles. Rather, the drawing of lines between speech and action; content and time-place-manner regulations; high- and low-value speech; and fighting words and words that are merely expressive will necessarily be *ad hoc* and context sensitive (1994: 130–1). This reflects the 'messy contingency of a world that defies the neatness of philosophical formulations', as well as the fact that free speech is not an independent value, but the name we give to verbal behaviour that serves our own agendas, a political trophy no longer of use once it has been captured by a politics in opposition to one's own (1994: 130, 102). Rather than attempting to furnish a list of unprotected utterances, I agree with Fish that it is better to inquire into the real-world impact of allowing certain forms of 'so-called speech to flourish' and proceed on the basis of this information (1994: 103, 125).

The information before us is that the attacks on and threats against women online breach laws, violate terms-of-agreement, and/or involve abuse, cruelty, and threats that would be regarded as entirely unacceptable in offline contexts. Cyber violence against women and girls is a form of violence that causes real harm. Further, failing to recognise this form of violence *as* violence gives further expression to and support for men's disproportionate share of the political, economic, and social power, as well as bolstering the culture of misogyny discussed in Chapter 2. Maybe the punishment for online violence should involve the withdrawal of certain online privileges (such as anonymity or access to certain platforms). Maybe it should involve fines, prosecutions in court, and/or imprisonment via existing laws or new legislation drafted specifically for this purpose. Either way, the point is that if gendered cyberhaters are too blizzardish, shark-like, or toddler-esque to regulate their own behaviour online, then institutions must step in and regulate it for them.

Notes

1   The World Wide Web Foundation's Web Index covers 86 countries and measures the web's contribution to social, economic and political progress.
2   I interviewed Lawder as part of my cyberhate research project.
3   While I acknowledge that citing material from the anonymous peer review process raises ethical questions, my case is that the two examples cited in this chapter provide critical insight into academic orientations which are usually concealed and which themselves have ethical implications. For me, therefore, citing them is the lesser evil.

4   The moral panic model is the idea that agents and institutions of control, including the media, exaggerate and amplify forms of deviance in order to justify the control of those portrayed as 'deviant' (Cohen, 2002).
5   My reading of 'SocJus' here is that it is short for 'social justice'.
6   For example, one dissenting contributor says attempting to get academics sacked is 'way off the mark of what GG [that is, GamerGate] stands for, and needs' (legayredditmodditors commenting beneath nochafaa, 2015).

CONCLUSION: THE ELECTRONIC EQUIVALENT OF EVERYWHERE

'Blow there and ... move your fingers up and down here'

Having identified a compelling and (relatively) new social problem, it is usual for books such as this one to offer solutions. In the case of gendered cyberhate – as with all complex problems – it is difficult to avoid sounding trite. How to end all these rape threats online? *Mais c'est très facile!* Simply convince the world that misogyny online is wrong, back this with appropriate law and platform reform, and everyone will use the internet happily ever after. While this prescription may be more or less apt, its gross simplification is reminiscent of the 1970s era Monty Python 'How to Do It' television skit in which a jaunty presenter devotes a full five seconds to teaching viewers how to play the flute: 'Well, here we are,' the John Cleese character enthuses. 'You blow there and you move your fingers up and down here.' As with the rest of the instructional advice offered in 'How to Do It' (the single segment also covers how to split the atom, how to construct box girder bridges, and how to irrigate the Sahara) the devil is obviously in the detail.

The same is true with any neatly packaged plan claiming to 'solve' gendered cyberhate. Firstly, this is truly a global problem in that it occurs throughout the world via mediums with scant regard for national boundaries. If we consider just one aspect of potential intervention – policy and law-making – the number of jurisdictions involved are so numerous and idiosyncratic that proposing a one-size-fits-all legislative solution would be entirely meaningless.

In the case of gendered cyberhate, the devil is also in the dynamism. The cybersphere is changing rapidly and can be wildly unpredictable. A young digital native may feel like Twitter has always been part of the social media landscape, yet it has only been delivering micro blogs to the masses since 2006. Consider, too, the mobile telephone revolution – another relatively new technological advance. Given the multitude of communication options permitted by these increasingly smart devices, who would have predicted that the sending of short, typed messages – reminiscent of telegrams – would prove so popular? That 'walk' lights at roads would need to be embedded in the ground to assist pedestrians glued to their phones (McGoogan, 2016)? Or that one of the unexpected consequences of the billions of text messages sent each month would be personal safety issues relating to the rise of not only 'sexting' but 'wexting' (that is, simultaneously walking and texting)? It is impossible to know what novel platform might next capture the public imagination, what unexpected consequences and social problems might arise, and what precise institutional interventions will be required to deal with the Next Big E-Thing.

In fact, there is a danger that even jurisdiction-specific remedies nutted out now may rapidly become obsolete and useless. The risk of sub-standard interventions is exacerbated by the high degree of media coverage given to problems relating to the internet and technology. This increases the pressure on regulators to succumb to penal populism (Roberts et al., 2003) and to make poorly considered decisions which may be ineffective or which create their own sets of unhelpful, unintended consequences. While policy-makers have been slow to respond to gendered cyberhate thus far, the issue is now in the international spotlight and a number of nations are clarifying existing legislation as well as considering new laws. We are at a critical juncture where the possibility for both success and failure are high.

The legal and technological minutiae of how authorities in various jurisdictions and venues handle gendered cyberhate are best left to experts in possession of local knowledge. Generally speaking, however, regulatory responses relating to new technologies must be savvy about existing systems, as well as possessing some flexibility in anticipation of changing circumstances (the buzz word is 'future proofing'). Moreover, they should be value sensitive. This term is used to describe the way ethics and values can be built into the earliest stages of the design and innovation process (Van den Hoven, 2013). It is also a useful concept to consider in jurisprudence, as well as when engaging in platform design and reform. A value sensitive approach would involve explicitly identifying and foregrounding the values we wish to cultivate before interventions are implemented. The goal here – and admittedly, it is a lofty, flute-ish one – is for regulators, platform managers, and tech designers to think as broadly and in as value-focused a way as possible while responses to gendered cyberhate are being considered and formulated. This would not entirely eliminate but might at least have the potential to reduce the risk of new measures whose shelf lives are short because they have come about as a result of knee-jerk decisions made during moments of media pressure.

Also, while gendered cyberhate is indeed playing out at the cutting edge of dynamic technological innovation, the androcentrism, sexism, and misogyny underpinning the phenomenon are old and depressingly predictable. Regardless of the novelty of future information and communications technology, it is highly likely that some or even many men will use it to derogate, oppress, and harass girls and women – at least so long as systemic inequities still dominate elsewhere. As such, the values regulators should be sensitive to when developing responses to the gendered cyberhate problem are gender equity values.

A glass half full of *déjà vu*

Over the course of this book I have used a combination of anecdotal evidence and empirical data to outline the history, nature, prevalence, and impact of gendered cyberhate. I have also explained why feminists fighting misogyny online are experiencing a profound sense of *déjà vu*. As with rape, domestic violence, and workplace sexual harassment prior to feminist campaigns in the 1970s, the abuse of girls and women online is routinely trivialised, mocked, dismissed as personal matters for individuals to solve, and presented as legally intractable. Also paralleling more 'traditional' forms of sexual assault and harassment is the way female targets are blamed, and male perpetrators are excused or quietly removed from the narrative altogether. Thus women are advised to take a multitude of 'safety' precautions online including avoiding commenting on or participating in debates about provocative political topics, taking care not to venture into unknown terrain or into conversations with unknown people, and refraining from posting images of themselves that male users might find too attractive (or too unattractive).

Time and again, multiple representatives of multiple institutions from multiple nations have failed to act on gendered cyberhate because targets are not believed or taken seriously, or because of lack of awareness / resources / leadership / legislation / interest / ability to recognise that online attackers are human beings with agency rather than blizzards, sharks, preschoolers, and so on. Time and again, women are blamed for the attacks against them, and offered the conflicting guidance that nothing happening online can cause 'real' harm, yet the internet is also a terribly dangerous place they should approach with extreme caution or avoid altogether. Time and again, the claimsmaking, rights, and experiences of perpetrators are protected and privileged. They're just stupid kids or immature men. They were just trying to be funny. They didn't realise what they were doing was wrong. They were engaging in important free speech. Oh, and if they don't turn out to be weather, a huge fish, or an infant, then some other person was probably using their computer that day that lady's vagina got threatened with pack incursion.

Maybe a dude who tells a woman he's going to decapitate her daughter and ejaculate in the stump *is* amusing himself and others. Maybe 'tits or GTFO' *is* a playful and 'ironic measure of deterrence' (Manivannan, 2013). Ultimately, however, the alleged or avowed intent of cyberhaters should not be privileged over the impact of their texts. Actual harm is what should count when determining how a putatively hostile online action should be appraised, and whether punitive measures should be taken against those responsible.

From a feminist perspective, it is dispiriting to witness not only the prevalence and noxiousness of gendered cyberhate, but the tenacious, seemingly activist-proof misogyny that continues metastasising throughout the broader culture. That feminist attempts to halt the flow of misogyny seem to serve merely as acts of displacement has a hydrodynamic/thermodynamic logic reminiscent of the arcade game Whac-A-Mole in that striking down one manifestation of misogyny is soon followed by the appearance of another form elsewhere (Jane, 2014b). Acknowledging the immensity of the battle is not to endorse giving up in despair, however, but to underline the pressing need to continue the mission. It offers orientation for future action, emphasises the importance of being realistic about the results likely to be achieved, and highlights the continuing importance of larger feminist projects.

'Smashing' is perhaps not the best verb to describe one's plan for the patriarchy if one's platform is anti-violence. Yet techno tinkering and new and improved laws will likely achieve little if we do not also address the patriarchal systems that continue to facilitate and constitute gender inequity and violence against women at the 'cellular' level of society. This does not mean we should wait for things to improve offline before taking action online. Instead, institutions and regulators must work together to apprehend individual offenders in online environments, *alongside* parallel campaigns to tackle structural misogyny. We may not be able to arrest our way out of the view that women are second-class citizens whose *raison d'être* is 'sperm receptacle', but it does not follow that no arrests should be made.

A glass half-full take on the sense of *déjà vu* outlined above is that feminists and civil rights activists have experience fighting very similar battles. Prior to the 1970s, sexual harassment and domestic violence were broadly accepted as personal practices and secret nuclear family business. Workplace sexual harassment was written off as harmless flirting, while domestic violence episodes were dismissed as nothing but lovers' quarrels (Hess, 2014). In the same way that feminists have tirelessly argued that rape and domestic violence are public crises rather than private problems, the abuse and harassment directed at girls and women online need to be addressed not as intimacy issues but as problems 'rooted in mechanisms of power and control' (Randol, 2005: 19).

I am gratified to report that an early version of this book began with an Alcoholics Anonymous-style 'admit there is a problem' as one of the first items on its agenda. Thanks largely to the awareness-raising efforts and advocacy work undertaken by gendered cyberhate targets and cyber feminists, the problem of misogyny online is now on the radar of international organisations such as the UN. Small but growing numbers of test cases are playing out in various courts, and some social media platforms are finally grinding into gear and making changes that might provide some assistance to targets. There is also an increasing awareness that the free speech argument mounted in defence of attackers does not hold water, partly because the speech rights of one group are being exercised at the expense of another. Indeed, no less than the Electronic Frontier Foundation (EFF) – an organisation with a strong free speech platform – has acknowledged that speaking out against online harassment is not censorship but a free speech-supporting gesture (Kayyali and O'Brien, 2015).

A paradoxical side-effect of the prevalence of violently gendered e-bile is that – like car crashes and cancer – the frequency with which it occurs can render it normalised and banal. Thus those of us who live much of our lives online have become skilled at 'seeing but not seeing' the rapey comments posted beneath YouTube fish tail braid clips, in much the same way that it has become possible to 'see but not see' the oddly punctuated emails from overfriendly Nigerian princes ever keen to share with us their impossibly large inheritances. Such habituated blindness, however, is not always an option for those targeted for the worst kinds of cyberhate and does nothing to address a problem that is not going away but is dramatically snowballing in size. In addition to causing direct harm, the effects of gendered cyberhate are insidious. If a young male user becomes accustomed to seeing female commentators threatened with rape after expressing their views on immigration, economic policy, or electronic dance music, it may well feel natural for him to follow suit. For targets, too, there is a boiling frog effect. Maybe the constant swirl of rape and death threats feels manageable, an unpleasant thing about which it is possible to become inured. But while the changes women are making in response to this material can be subtle on a daily basis, together they constitute large changes over time. We need to reverse engineer the normalisation process that has occurred around gendered cyberhate and to engage in a 'grisly process of re-sensitisation' on par with recovering one's sense of smell or taste (Ellen, 2015).

We also need to remember that awareness ≠ action. The UN Broadband Commission report on cyber VAWG includes a wry remark by a security expert who says: 'We hear about wake-up calls, but people keep hitting the snooze button' (Winkler cited in 'Cyber violence against women and girls: A world-wide wake-up call', 2015: 8). This snooze button must be permanently disabled. Framing the internet as a virtual Wild West where the usual laws do not apply or simply *cannot* be applied was understandable in the earliest days of the web. But the cybersphere is no longer a new frontier or optional extra. It is a not-negotiable part of contemporary life and citizenship: the place where people go to complete the most mundane of daily activities – banking, bill paying, and sub-floor ventilation shopping. This is not the electronic equivalent of an Everest base camp where only those who possess elite training, elaborate safety equipment, and a willingness to sacrifice personal safety for the mission should explore. It is the electronic equivalent of everywhere. As such, the price of entry should never include being called ugly, fat, and slutty and threatened with rape by men whose all caps-claim is that there is no misogyny on the internet.

After all, the public cybersphere isn't actually public if half the people are being told to get the fuck out.

REFERENCES

Aedy, R. (2013) 'A journalist's guide to finding the truth via social media', *Radio National* (radio broadcast), 5 December, available at: http://www.abc.net.au/radionational/programs/mediareport/spotting-the-fakes2c-the-no-nothings-and-the-too-good-to-be-tr/5134456 (accessed 4/7/16).

'AFP staff statistics' (2016) *Australian Federal Police*, available at: http://www.afp.gov.au/media-centre/facts-stats/afp-staff-statistics (accessed 1/5/16).

Alexander, L. (2015) 'SXSW's GamerGate debacle shows it's clueless on diversity', *Wired*, 28 October, available at http://www.wired.com/2015/10/sxsw-diversity-gamergate/ (accessed 29/12/15).

Angelari, M. (1993) 'Hate crime statutes: A promising tool for fighting violence against women', *Journal of Gender & the Law* 2(63): 63–105.

Ankucic, M. (2015) 'Academia's anti-gaming hysteria: A conversation with Sara Rahman', *The Viking Gamer*, 23 July, available at: https://thevikinggamer.wordpress.com/2015/07/23/academias-anti-gaming-hysteria-a-conversation-with-sara-rahman/ (accessed 20/6/16).

Auernheimer, A. (2013) 'Of Sierras and Sandovals', *Pastebin*, 28 September, available at: http://pastebin.com/DUWEZfTy (accessed 18/10/13).

'Australian media still a Blokesworld in 2016' (2016) *Media, Entertainment and Arts Alliance*, 6 March, available at: https://www.meaa.org/news/australian-media-still-a-blokesworld-in-2016/ (accessed 13/4/16).

Bacchiocchi, G. (2016) '"Making a Murderer" prosecutor target of death & rape threats!', *Radar*, 4 February, available at: http://radaronline.com/celebrity-news/making-a-murderer-steven-avery-prosecutor-death-threats-trolls-threaten-rape-daughter/ (accessed 6/2/16).

Badham, V. (2015) 'A man lost his job for harassing a woman online? Good', *The Guardian*, 2 December, available at: http://www.theguardian.com/commentisfree/2015/dec/02/a-man-lost-his-job-for-harassing-a-woman-online-good (accessed 16/12/15).

Barker, C., and Jane, E. A. (2016) *Cultural Studies: Theory and Practice*, 5th edn. Los Angeles: Sage.

Barlow, J. P. (1996) 'A Declaration of the Independence of Cyberspace', *Electronic Frontier Foundation*, available at: https://projects.eff.org/~barlow/Declaration-Final.html (accessed 5/4/15).

Bartlett, J., Norrie, R., Patel, S., Rumpel, R., and Wibberley, S. (2014) 'Misogyny on Twitter', *Demos*, May, available at: http://www.demos.co.uk/files/MISOGYNY_ON_TWITTER.pdf?1399567516 (accessed 2/6/16).

Battersby, L. (2013) 'Twitter criticised for failing to respond to Caroline Criado-Perez rape threats', *The Sydney Morning Herald*, 29 July, available at: http://www.smh.com.au/digital-life/digital-life-news/twitter-criticised-for-failing-to-respond-to-caroline-criadoperez-rape-threats-20130729-2qu8d.html (accessed 18/12/15).

Baudrillard, J. (2001) *Selected Writings – 2nd edition revised and expanded*. Edited and introduced by M. Poster. Stanford, CA: Stanford University Press.

Beard, M. (2013) 'Internet fury: Or having your anatomy dissected online', *The Times Literary Supplement*, 27 January, available at: http://timesonline.typepad.com/dons_life/2013/01/internet-fury.html (accessed 27/2/2016).

Beirich, H. (2014) 'White homicide worldwide', *Southern Poverty Law Center*, available at: www.splcenter.org/sites/default/files/d6_legacy_files/downloads/publication/white-homicide-worldwide.pdf (accessed 22/8/15).

Bilton, N. (2010) 'One on one: Christopher Poole, founder of 4chan', *The New York Times*, 19 March, available at: http://bits.blogs.nytimes.com/2010/03/19/one-on-one-christopher-poole-founder-of-4chan/ (accessed 2/1/16).

Black Poison Soul (2014) 'Tits or GTFO', *Black Poison Soul*, 5 June, available at: http://blackpoisonsoul.blogspot.com.au/2014/06/tits-or-gtfo.html (accessed 21/6/16).

Blunden, M. (2015) 'Caroline Criado-Perez: How I won my banknote battle ... and defied rape threat trolls', *Evening Standard*, 27 November, available at: http://www.standard.co.uk/news/london/caroline-criadoperez-how-i-won-my-banknote-battle-and-defied-rape-threat-trolls-a3123956.html (accessed 1/12/15).

Bokhari, A. (2015) 'Gamergate: A year in review', *Breitbart*, 15 September, available at: http://www.breitbart.com/big-journalism/2015/09/15/gamergate-a-year-in-review/ (accessed 28/12/15).

Borchers, C., and Keohane, D. (2015) 'Citing threats, game maker pulls her company from PAX East fest', *Boston Globe*, 24 February, available at: https://www.bostonglobe.com/business/2015/02/24/pax-east-withdrawal-reveals-sexist-side-video-game-culture/SiRAzMnuI6iea0woo9ob6I/story.html (accessed 27/1/16).

Bort, J. (2016) 'One of Docker's star engineers got so many death and rape threats, the company hired private detectives to protect her', *Business Insider Australia*, 26 April, available at: http://www.businessinsider.com.au/death-rape-threats-for-docker-engineer-2016-4?r=US&IR=T (accessed 26/4/16).

Braman, S. (2011) 'Internet policy', in M. Consalvo and C. Ess (eds.), *The Handbook of Internet Studies*. West Sussex: Wiley-Blackwell.

Brown, L. (ed.) (1993) *The New Shorter Oxford English Dictionary on Historical Principles – Volume 1: A–M*. Oxford: Clarendon Press.

Brown, T. (2012) 'Charlotte's hell', *60 Minutes*, 31 August, available at: http://sixtyminutes.ninemsn.com.au/article.aspx?id=8525498 (accessed 11/1/16).

Buchanan, E. A. (2011) 'Internet research ethics: Past, present, and future', in M. Consalvo and C. Ess (eds.), *The Handbook of Internet Studies*. Oxford: Wiley-Blackwell.

Buchwald, E., Fletcher, P. R., and Roth, M. (eds.) (1993) *Transforming a Rape Culture*. Minneapolis: Milkweed Editions.

Buckels, E. E., Trapnell, P. D., and Paulhus, D. L. (2014) 'Trolls just want to have fun', *Personality and Individual Differences* 67: 97–102.

Butler, D., and Moseley, L. (2013) *Explain Pain, 2nd edn.* Adelaide: Noigroup Publications.

'By the numbers' (2016) *National Center for Women & Information Technology*, 10 March, available at: https://www.ncwit.org/resources/numbers (accessed 1/5/16).

Carter, C. (2014) 'Twitter troll jailed for "campaign of hatred" against Stella Creasy', *The Telegraph*, 29 March, available at: http://www.telegraph.co.uk/news/uknews/crime/11127808/Twitter-troll-jailed-for-campaign-of-hatred-against-Stella-Creasy.html (accessed 7/3/16).

Cavendish, D. (2013) 'Steven Berkoff: Thousands support my views on Twitter', *The Telegraph*, 12 August, available at: http://www.telegraph.co.uk/culture/theatre/edinburgh-festival/10233683/Steven-Berkoff-Thousands-support-my-views-on-Twitter.html (accessed 20/3/16).

Chalmers, M. (2015) '"The best thing about feminists is they don't get action so when you rape them it's 100 times tighter": Welcome to Facebook and Tinder', *New Matilda*, 28 August, available at: https://newmatilda.com/2015/08/28/best-thing-about-feminists-they-dont-get-action-so-when-you-rape-them-its-100-times/ (accessed 14/6/16).

Chasmar, J. (2015) 'Justin Moed, Democratic lawmaker, "truly sorry" for sexting Sydney Leathers of Weiner scandal', *The Washington Times*, 11 March, available at: http://www.washingtontimes.com/news/2015/mar/11/justin-moed-democratic-lawmaker-truly-sorry-for-se/ (accessed 29/6/16).

'Cheerleader falls on her face in front of the school' (2008) *Nothing Toxic*, 14 January, available at http://www.nothingtoxic.com/media/1200291750/Cheerleader_Falls_on_her_Face_in_Front_of_the_School (accessed 13/1/2009).

Chen, A. (2012a) 'Unmasking Reddit's Violentacrez, the biggest troll on the web', *Gawker*, 12 October, available at: http://gawker.com/5950981/unmasking-reddits-violentacrez-the-biggest-troll-on-the-web (accessed 2/1/16).

Chen, A. (2012b) 'Reddit's biggest troll fired from his real-world job; Reddit continues to censor Gawker articles', *Gawker*, 15 October, available at: http://gawker.com/5951987/reddits-biggest-troll-fired-from-his-real-world-job-reddit-continues-to-censor-gawker-articles (accessed 22/6/16).

Citron, D. K. (2014a) *Hate Crimes in Cyberspace.* Cambridge, MA: Harvard University Press.

Citron, D. K. (2014b) '"Revenge porn" should be a crime in U.S.', *CNN*, 16 January, available at: http://edition.cnn.com/2013/08/29/opinion/citron-revenge-porn/ (accessed 16/1/16).

Citron, D. K. (2014c) 'How cyber mobs and trolls have ruined the internet – and destroyed lives', *Newsweek*, 19 September, available at: http://www.newsweek.com/internet-and-golden-age-bully-271800 (accessed 14/1/16).

Citron, D. K., and Franks, M. A. (2014) 'Criminalizing revenge porn', *Wake Forest Law Review* 49, 19 May: 345–391, available at: http://digitalcommons.law.umaryland.edu/cgi/viewcontent.cgi?article=2424&context=fac_pubs (accessed 4/7/16).

Clark, K. (2015) 'Sexism in cyberspace', *The Hill*, 10 March, available at: http://thehill.com/opinion/op-ed/235070-sexism-in-cyberspace (accessed 21/3/16).

Cockerell, J. (2014) 'Twitter "trolls" Isabella Sorley and John Nimmo jailed for abusing feminist campaigner Caroline Criado-Perez', *Independent*, 25 January, available at: http://www.independent.co.uk/news/uk/crime/twitter-trolls-isabella-sorley-and-john-nimmo-jailed-for-abusing-feminist-campaigner-caroline-criado-9083829.html (accessed 5/2/16).

Cohen, S. (2002) *Folk Devils and Moral Panics*, 3rd edition. London: Routledge.

Coleman, E. G. (2012) 'Phreaks, hackers, and trolls: The politics of transgression and spectacle', in M. Mandiberg (ed.), *The Social Media Reader*. New York: New York University Press.

'Collective Shout' (n.d.) *Collective Shout*, available at: http://www.collectiveshout.org/ (accessed 10/1/16).

Colvin, M., and Mark, D. (2012) 'TV presenter in hospital after vicious Twitter attacks', *PM*, 30 August, available at: http://www.abc.net.au/pm/content/2012/s3579714.htm (accessed 11/1/16).

Consalvo, M., and Ess, C. (2011) *The Handbook of Internet Studies*. West Sussex: Wiley-Blackwell.

Cooper, R. (2014) 'How to stop misogynists from terrorizing the world of gamers', *The Week*, 2 September, available at: http://theweek.com/articles/444093/how-stop-misogynists-from-terrorizing-world-gamers (accessed 3/1/16).

Corbett, C., and Hill, C. (2015) 'Solving the equation: The variables for women's success in engineering and computing', *American Association of University Women*, March, available at: http://www.aauw.org/files/2015/03/Solving-the-Equation-report-nsa.pdf (accessed 30/6/16).

Cranston, H. (2015) 'This is what it's like to have a vagina on the internet', *The Huffington Post*, 30 December, available at: http://www.huffingtonpost.com/hannah-cranston/this-is-what-its-like-to-have-a-vagina-on-the-internet_b_8808742.html (accessed 19/7/16).

Creasy, S. (2013) '@stellacreasy', *Twitter*, 29 July, available at: https://twitter.com/stellacreasy/status/361778205704720384 (accessed 14/6/16).

Criado-Perez, C. (2013) 'She called the police. They said that there was nothing they could do', *Mamamia*, 14 November, available at: http://www.mamamia.com.au/caroline-criado-perez-cyber-harassment-speech/ (accessed 11/1/16).

Criado-Perez, C. (2016) 'When it comes to online abuse, we need to see a fuller picture', *The Pool*, 1 June, available at: https://www.the-pool.com/news-views/opinion/2016/22/caroline-criado-perez-on-demos-and-online-abuse (accessed 16/6/16).

Crooke, C. (2013) 'Women in law enforcement', *COPS*, available at: http://cops.usdoj.gov/html/dispatch/07-2013/women_in_law_enforcement.asp (accessed 1/5/16).

Crossley-Holland, D. (executive producer) (2010) *The Virtual Revolution* (television series). Originally broadcast on the BBC from 30 January to 20 February.

'Cyber violence against women and girls: A world-wide wake-up call' (2015) *The United Nations Broadband Commission for Digital Development Working Group on Broadband and Gender*, available at http://www.unwomen.org/~/media/headquarters/attachments/sections/library/publications/2015/cyber_violence_gender%20report.pdf (accessed 14/12/15).

Dale, J. (2016) 'The scale of online misogyny', *Demos*, 26 May, available at: http://www.demos.co.uk/blog/misogyny-online/ (accessed 2/6/16).

Davis, K. (2016) 'Personal injury lawyers turn to neuroscience to back claims of chronic pain', *ABA Journal*, 1 March, available at: http://www.abajournal.com/magazine/article/personal_injury_lawyers_turn_to_neuroscience_to_back_claims_of_chronic_pain (accessed 5/6/16).

Day, F. (2014) 'Crossing the street', *feliciaday.com*, 22 October, available at: http://feliciaday.com/blog/crossing-the-street/ (accessed 25/6/16).

Dillon, C. (2016) '#MoreThanMean: Viral video opens debate about online trolling against women', *DW*, 28 April, available at: http://www.dw.com/en/morethanmean-viral-video-opens-debate-about-online-trolling-against-women/a-19223194 (accessed 29/6/16).

Di Stefano, M. (2015) 'Tyler, The Creator called out a feminist activist on Twitter and the results are not surprising', *BuzzFeed*, 28 July, available at: http://www.buzzfeed.com/markdistefano/an-odd-future#.jcQJg4Ozzg (accessed 10/1/16).

'Domestic legal remedies for technology-related violence against women: Review of related studies and literature' (2014) *Association for Progressive Communications*, May, available at: http://www.genderit.org/sites/default/upload/domestic_legal_remedies_for_technology-related_violence_against_women_review_of_related_studies_and_literature.pdf (accessed 28/1/16).

Douglas, K. M. (2008) 'Antisocial communication on electronic mail and the internet', in E. A. Konijin, S. Utz, M. Tanis and S. B. Barnes (eds.), *Mediated Interpersonal Communication*. London: Routledge.

Dowell, B. (2013) 'Mary Beard row: Website owner says sorry but accuses friends of "trolling"', *The Guardian*, 25 January, available at: http://www.theguardian.com/media/2013/jan/25/mary-beard-row-website-apologises (accessed 27/2/16).

Doyle, S. (2011a) 'Why are you in such a bad mood? #MenCallMeThings responds!', *Tiger Beatdown*, 7 November, available at: http://tigerbeatdown.com/2011/11/07/why-are-you-in-such-a-bad-mood-mencallmethings-responds/ (accessed 10/1/16).

Doyle, S. (2011b) 'But how do you know its sexist? The #MenCallMeThings round-up', *Tiger Beatdown*, 10 November, available at: http://tigerbeatdown.com/2011/11/10/but-how-do-you-know-its-sexist-the-mencallmethings-round-up/ (accessed 21/12/15).

Doyle, S. (2011c) 'The girl's guide to staying safe online', *In These Times*, 17 November, available at: https://www.inthesetimes.com/article/12311/the_girls_guide_to_staying_safe_online/ (accessed 9/12/15).

dude, A. (2008) 'Owned', *Urban Dictionary*, 2 December, available at: http://www.urbandictionary.com/define.php?term=Owned (accessed 11/12/15).

Duff, E. (2016) '"Satanic" sergeant suspended for posting degrading slurs before Greens MP Jenny Leong harassed', *The Age*, 17 April, available at: http://www.theage.com.au/nsw/nsw-police-sergeant-posted-homopho-bic-sexually-degrading-slurs-before-greens-mp-jenny-leong-was-harassed-20160415-go7kyj.html (accessed 18/4/16).

Duggan, M. (2014) 'Online harassment', *Pew Research Center*, 22 October, available at: http://www.pewinternet.org/2014/10/22/online-harassment/ (accessed 4/1/16).

Duggan, M. (2015) 'Gaming and gamers', *Pew Research Center*, 15 December, available at: http://www.pewinternet.org/2015/12/15/gaming-and-gamers/ (accessed 4/1/16).

Dutton, W. H. (ed.) (2013) *The Oxford Handbook of Internet Studies*. Oxford: Oxford University Press.

Edwards, K. (2013) 'Trolling #TellAFeministThankYou', *Daily Life*, 13 February, available at: http://www.dailylife.com.au/news-and-views/dl-opinion/troll-ing-tellafeministthankyou-20130213-2ecoz.html (accessed 27/12/15).

Elam, P. (2011) 'Stalking Sady Doyle', *A Voice for Men*, 18 November, available at: http://www.avoiceformen.com/feminism/feminist-lies-feminism/stalking-sady-doyle/ (accessed 9/12/15).

Ellen, B. (2015) 'Let's never get inured to online rape threats', *The Guardian*, 1 November, available at: http://www.theguardian.com/commentisfree/2015/nov/01/online-rape-threats-jess-phillips (accessed 2/1/16).

Elliot, A. (2015) 'Gamergate: Gender at work in the new economy', 3 August, seminar, School of Social and Political Sciences, The University of Sydney.

Elliott, C. (2011) 'Facebook is fine with hate speech, as long as it's directed at women', *The Guardian*, 4 October, available at: http://www.theguardian.com/commentisfree/2011/oct/04/facebook-hate-speech-women-rape (accessed 14/3/16).

Elliott, T. (2016) 'Fat, frocked up and fighting back', *The Sydney Morning Herald Good Weekend*, 23 January, available at: http://www.smh.com.au/good-weekend/fat-frocked-up-and-fighting-back-20151207-glhlg7.html (accessed 24/6/16).

Evans, K. (2011) 'Men call me things: it's not as romantic as it sounds', *The Drum*, 11 November, available at: http://www.abc.net.au/unleashed/3659712.html (accessed 13/1/16).

'Facts and figures: Leadership and political participation' (2016) *UN Women*, January, available at: http://www.unwomen.org/en/what-we-do/leadership-and-political-participation/facts-and-figures (accessed 28/1/16).

Feinberg, J. (1985) *Offense to Others: The Moral Limits of the Criminal Law*. Oxford: Oxford University Press.

Finley, K. (2016) 'Want to save the comments from trolls? Do it yourself', *Wired*, 18 March, available at http://www.wired.com/2016/03/want-save-comments-trolls/ (accessed 29/3/16).

Fish, S. E. (1994) *There's No Such Thing as Free Speech: And It's a Good Thing, Too*. New York: Oxford University Press.

Flew, T. (2004) *New Media: An Introduction*. South Melbourne: Oxford University Press.

Flynn, C. (2016) 'The "Inside Amy Schumer" sketch about internet trolling is frighteningly realistic', *Bustle*, 29 May, available at: http://www.bustle.com/articles/157723-the-inside-amy-schumer-sketch-about-internet-trolling-is-frighteningly-realistic (accessed 1/5/16).

Ford, C. (2015) 'Good guys don't play nice', *Fight Like A Girl*, 25 November, available at: http://clementinefordwriter.blogspot.com.au/2015/11/good-guys-dont-play-nice.html (accessed 30/11/15).

Forrest, H. (2015) 'SXSW announces March 12 online harassment summit [updated 11.17.2015]', *SXSW*, 30 October, available at: http://www.sxsw.com/news/2015/sxsw-announces-march-12-online-harassment-summit (accessed 3/2/16).

Frazelle, J. (2015) 'This industry is fucked', *Jessie Frazelle's Blog*, 5 July, available at: https://blog.jessfraz.com/post/this-industry-is-fucked/ (accessed 26/4/16).

Gardiner, B., Mansfield, M., Anderson, I., Holder, J., Louter, D., and Ulmanu, M. (2016) 'The dark side of Guardian comments', *The Guardian*, 12 April, available at: https://www.theguardian.com/technology/2016/apr/12/the-dark-side-of-guardian-comments (accessed 13/4/16).

Gaudiosi, J. (2014) '10 powerful women in video games', *Fortune*, 23 September, available at: http://fortune.com/2014/09/23/10-powerful-women-video-games/ (accessed 1/5/16).

Gjoni, E. (2014) *thezoepost*, 16 August, available at: https://thezoepost.wordpress.com/ (accessed 28/12/15).

Glukhov, G. V., and Martynova, I. A. (2015) 'Efficiency of threats in interpersonal communication', *Review of European Studies* 7(9): 60–67.

Goddard, S. L. (2015) 'Techno-womanism: A moral imperative for social justice, faith, and the digital space', unpublished master's thesis, Union Theological Seminary, 10 April, available at: http://dx.doi.org/10.7916/D8RB73HX (accessed 16/6/16).

Gold, T. (2013) 'How do we tackle online rape threats?', *The Guardian*, 29 July, available at: http://www.theguardian.com/commentisfree/2013/jul/28/how-to-tackle-online-rape-threats (accessed 2/1/16).

Goldberg, M. (2015) 'Feminist writers are so besieged by online abuse that some have begun to retire', *The Washington Post*, 20 February, available at: https://www.washingtonpost.com/opinions/online-feminists-increasingly-ask-are-the-psychic-costs-too-much-to-bear/2015/02/19/3dc4ca6c-b7dd-11e4-a200-c008a01a6692_story.html (accessed 14/1/16).

Good, O. (2011) 'Well, that's one way to combat misogyny in gaming', *Kotaku*, 23 July, available at: http://kotaku.com/5824084/well-thats-one-way-to-combat-misogyny-in-gaming (accessed 3/2/16).

Graham, G., and Henry, R. (2013) 'Meet the Caesar of suburban poison', *The Sunday Times*, 27 January, available at: http://www.thesundaytimes.co.uk/sto/news/article1202533.ece (accessed 27/6/16).

Greenhouse, E. (2013) 'Twitter's free-speech problem', *The New Yorker*, 1 August, available at: http://www.newyorker.com/online/blogs/elements/2013/08/how-free-should-speech-be-on-twitter.html (accessed 28/12/15).

'"Grow up" and stop taking naked photos of yourself, police tell revenge porn inquiry' (2016) *The Guardian*, available at: http://www.theguardian.com/australia-news/2016/feb/18/grow-up-and-stop-taking-naked-photos-of-yourself-says-senior-police-officer (accessed 26/2/16).

Hardaker, C. (2016) 'Misogyny, machines, and the media, or: how science should not be reported', *Dr Claire Hardaker*, 27 May, available at: http://wp.lancs.ac.uk/drclaireh/2016/05/27/misogyny-machines-and-the-media-or-how-science-should-not-be-reported/ (accessed 2/6/16).

Harris, M. (2015) Facebook post. Available via ABCNews23's Timeline Photos, available at: https://www.facebook.com/ABCNews23/photos/a.4868214780 74780.1073741827.486818034741791/857180784372179/ (accessed 1/12/15).

Hasham, N. (2016) 'Woman whose partner coerced her into sex with prostitute felt like "performing donkey", inquiry told', *The Sydney Morning Herald*, 19 January, available at: http://www.smh.com.au/federal-politics/political-news/woman-whose-partner-coerced-her-into-sex-with-prostitute-felt-like-performing-donkey-inquiry-told-20160119-gm8ubb.html (accessed 23/1/16).

Henry, N. (2015) 'Factbox: Revenge porn laws in Australia and beyond', *SBS*, 13 July, available at: http://www.sbs.com.au/news/dateline/article/2015/07/13/factbox-revenge-porn-laws-australia-and-beyond (accessed 2/5/16).

Henry, N., and Powell, A. (2015) 'Embodied harms: Gender, shame, and technology-facilitated sexual violence', *Violence Against Women*: 21(6): 758–799. DOI: 10.1177/1077801215576581.

Hern, A. (2014) 'Felicia Day's public details put online after she described Gamergate fears', *The Guardian*, 23 October, available at: https://www.theguardian.com/technology/2014/oct/23/felicia-days-public-details-online-gamergate (accessed 25/6/16).

Hernandez, C. (2015) 'Solidarity with @CoralieAlison', *End Online Misogyny*, 28 July, available at: http://www.endmisogyny.org/soldiarity-with-coraliealison/ (accessed 5/1/16).

Hess, A. (2014) 'Why women aren't welcome on the internet', *Pacific Standard*, 6 January, available at: http://www.psmag.com/health-and-behavior/women-arent-welcome-internet-72170 (accessed 17/12/15).

Hunsinger, J., Klastrup, L., and Allen, M. (2010) *International Handbook of Internet Research*. Dordrecht: Springer.

'If someone walked up and said, "I'm going to rape you", you'd ring 999: Stella Creasy fights the Twitter trolls' (2013) *Evening Standard*, 30 July, available at: http://www.standard.co.uk/lifestyle/london-life/if-someone-walked-up-and-said-i-m-going-to-rape-you-you-d-ring-999-stella-creasy-fights-the-twitter-8737796.html (accessed 14/6/16).

Imran, R. (2005) 'Legal injustices: The Zina Hudood Ordinance of Pakistan and its implications for women', *Journal of International Women's Studies* 7(2): 78–100.

'Ironic porn purchase leads to unironic ejaculation' (1999) *The Onion*, 1 December, available at: http://www.theonion.com/article/ironic-porn-purchase-leads-to-unironic-ejaculation-1567 (accessed 9/5/16).

Jackman, C. (2011) 'War of words', *The Australian,* 4 June, available at: http://www.theaustralian.com.au/life/weekend-australian-magazine/war-of-words/story-e6frg8h6-1226068173588 (accessed 22/2/15).

Jane, E. A. (2014a) '"Your a ugly, whorish, slut": Understanding e-bile', *Feminist Media Studies* 14(4): 531–546.

Jane, E. A. (2014b) '"Back to the kitchen, cunt": Speaking the unspeakable about online misogyny', *Continuum: Journal of Media & Cultural Studies* 28(4): 558–570. DOI: 10.1080/10304312.2014.924479.

Jane, E. A. (2014c) 'The scapegoating of cheerleading and cheerleaders', in J. Hodge, S. Cowdell, and C. Fleming (eds.), *Violence, Desire, and the Sacred: René Girard and Sacrifice in Life, Love, and Literature.* New York: Bloomsbury.

Jane, E. A. (2014d) 'Beyond antifandom: Cheerleading, textual hate and new media ethics', *International Journal of Cultural Studies* 17(2): 175–190. DOI: 10.1177/1367877913514330.

Jane, E. A. (2015) 'Flaming? What flaming? The pitfalls and potentials of researching online hostility', *Ethics and Information Technology* 17(1): 65–87.

Jane, E. A. (2016a) '"Dude ... stop the spread": Antagonism, agonism, and #manspreading on social media', *International Journal of Cultural Studies.* DOI: 10.1177/1367877916637151

Jane, E. A. (2016b) 'Online misogyny and feminist digilantism', *Continuum: Journal of Media & Cultural Studies,* published online 31 March, available at: http://dx.doi.org/10.1080/10304312.2016.1166560 (accessed 3/4/16).

Jane, E. A. (2016c [forthcoming]) 'Feminist digilante responses to a slut-shaming on Facebook', *Social Media + Society,* accepted for publication on 31 January, 2016.

Jason, Z. (2015) 'Game of fear', *Boston Magazine,* May, available at: http://www.bostonmagazine.com/news/article/2015/04/28/gamergate/ (accessed 28/12/15).

Jenson, J., and de Castell, S. (2013) 'Tipping points: Marginality, misogyny and videogames', *Journal of Curriculum Theorizing* 29(2): 72–85.

Jeong, S. (2016) 'Parody account mocks Twitter for not suspending harassers, gets suspended', *Motherboard,* 3 February, available at: http://motherboard.vice.com/read/parody-account-mocks-twitter-for-not-suspending-harassers-gets-suspended (accessed 6/2/16).

'Jon Stewart's wife Tracey is overweight, unattractive' (2011) *Mofo Politics,* 8 March, available at: http://www.mofopolitics.com/2011/03/08/jon-stewarts-wife-tracey-is-overweight-unattractive/ (accessed 9/12/11).

Jouvenal, J. (2013) 'Stalkers use online ads as weapon against victims', *The Washington Post,* 14 July, available at: https://www.washingtonpost.com/local/i-live-in-fear-of-anyone-coming-to-my-door/2013/07/14/26c11442-e359-11e2-aef3-339619eab080_story.html (accessed 7/1/16).

Judd, A. (2015) 'Forget your team: Your online violence toward girls and women is what can kiss my ass', *mic.com,* 19 March, available at: http://mic.com/articles/113226/forget-your-team-your-online-violence-toward-girls-and-women-is-what-can-kiss-my-ass#.qJqSw1ick (accessed 2/1/16).

Kaufer, D. (2000) *Flaming: A White Paper.* Pittsburgh, PA: Department of English, Carnegie Mellon University.

Kayyali, D., and O'Brien, D. (2015) 'Facing the challenge of online harassment', *Electronic Frontier Foundation*, 8 January, available at: https://www.eff.org/deeplinks/2015/01/facing-challenge-online-harassment (25/3/16).

Kluwe, C. (2014) 'Why #Gamergaters piss me the f*** off', *The Cauldron*, 21 October, available at: https://thecauldron.si.com/why-gamergaters-piss-me-the-f-off-a7e4c7f6d8a6#.tp97najjj (accessed 25/6/16).

Knowles, R. (2011) 'Facebook "rape" page to stay despite charity criticism', *BBC*, 7 October, available at: http://www.bbc.co.uk/newsbeat/article/15130624/facebook-rape-page-to-stay-despite-charity-criticism (accessed 5/3/16).

Koopman, C. (2013) *Genealogy as Critique: Foucault and the Problems of Modernity.* Bloomington: Indiana University Press.

Kritzman, L. D. (ed.) (1988) *Michel Foucault: Politics, Philosophy, Culture: Interviews and Other Writings, 1977–1984.* London: Routledge.

Kuntsman, A. (2007) 'Belonging through violence: Flaming, erasure, and performativity in queer migrant community', in K. O'Riordan and D. J. Phillips (eds.), *Queer Online: Media Technology & Sexuality.* New York: Peter Lang.

Lachenal, J. (2016) 'Tweet leads to rape threats, parody Twitter support account suspended, Twitter is an awful dumpster fire', *The Mary Sue*, 4 February, available at: http://www.themarysue.com/twitter-is-awful/ (accessed 6/2/16).

Landers, C. (n.d.) 'Serious business: Anonymous takes on Scientology (and doesn't afraid of anything)', *Chris Landers* (originally published in *Baltimore Citypaper*), available at: http://www.chrislanders.net/serious-business/ (accessed 23/6/16).

Lange, P. G. (2006) 'What is your claim to flame?', *First Monday* 11(9), 4 September, available at: http://firstmonday.org/ojs/index.php/fm/article/view/1393/1311 (accessed 24/12/2013).

Lange, P. G. (2007) 'Commenting on comments: Investigating responses to antagonism on YouTube', *Society for Applied Anthropology Conference*, Tampa, Florida.

Laville, S. (2016) 'Online abuse: "existing laws too fragmented and don't serve victims"', *The Guardian*, 5 March, available at: http://www.theguardian.com/uk-news/2016/mar/04/online-abuse-existing-laws-too-fragmented-and-dont-serve-victims-says-police-chief (accessed 13/4/16).

Lea, M., O'Shea, T., Fung, P., and Spears, R. (1992) '"Flaming" in computer-mediated communication: Observations, explanations, implications', in M. Lea (ed.), *Contexts of Computer-Mediated Communication.* Hertfordshire: Harvester Wheatsheaf.

Lee, A. (2014) '#Gamergate: The new face of misogynist terrorism', *Daylight Atheism*, 20 October, available at: http://www.patheos.com/blogs/daylightatheism/2014/10/gamergate-the-new-face-of-misogynist-terrorism/ (accessed 3/2/16).

Lee, H. (2005) 'Behavioral strategies for dealing with flaming in an online forum', *The Sociological Quarterly* 46(2): 385–403. DOI: 10.1111/j.1533-8525.2005.00017.x.

Lenssen, P. (2007) 'A chat with Aaron Swartz', *Google Blogoscoped*, 7 May, available at: http://blogoscoped.com/archive/2007-05-07-n78.html (accessed 29/3/16).

Lessig, L. (2007) 'Keen's "The Cult of the Amateur": BRILLIANT!', *Lessig*, 31 May, available at: www.lessig.org/2007/05/keens-the-cult-of-the-amateur/ (accessed 22/1/16).

Lewis, H. (2011) '"You should have your tongue ripped out": The reality of sexist abuse online', *NewStatesman*, 3 November, available at: http://www.newstatesman.com/blogs/helen-lewis-hasteley/2011/11/comments-rape-abuse-women (accessed 23/12/15).

Lewis, H. (2012) 'This is what online harassment looks like', *NewStatesman*, 6 July, available at: http://www.newstatesman.com/blogs/internet/2012/07/what-online-harassment-looks (accessed 27/12/15).

Lewis, H. (2013) 'Who are the trolls?', *NewStatesman*, 29 July, available at http://www.newstatesman.com/helen-lewis/2013/07/who-are-trolls (accessed 27/1/16).

Lyons, K. (2014) '"I got thousands of death and rape threats and the police just laughed at me": The anti-violence campaigner who was afraid to leave her house after she stood up to superstar rappers over their offensive lyrics', *Daily Mail Australia*, 23 June, available at: http://www.dailymail.co.uk/news/article-2665594/I-got-thousands-death-rape-threats-police-just-laughed-The-anti-violence-campaigner-afraid-leave-house-threatened-rappers-fans.html (accessed 10/1/16).

Maatz, L. (2015) 'Hate crimes can be motivated by gender bias, but there are tools to address them', *The Huffington Post*, 3 November, available at: http://www.huffingtonpost.com/lisa-maatz/hate-crimes-can-be-motiva_b_8462856.html (accessed 29/3/16).

McCosker, A. (2013) 'Trolling as provocation: YouTube's agonistic publics', *Convergence: The International Journal of Research into New Media Technologies* 20(2): 201–217. DOI: 10.1177/1354856513501413.

McGoogan, C. (2016) 'German city installs traffic lights in pavements to protect texting pedestrians', *The Telegraph*, 26 April, available at: http://www.telegraph.co.uk/technology/2016/04/26/german-city-installs-traffic-lights-in-pavements-to-protect-text/ (accessed 5/5/16).

McKee, H. (2002) '"YOUR VIEWS SHOWED TRUE IGNORANCE!!!": (Mis)Communication in an online interracial discussion forum', *Computers and Composition* 19: 411–434.

McKenna, K. Y. A., and Bargh, J. A. (2000) 'Plan 9 from Cyberspace: The implications of the internet for personality and social psychology', *Personality and Social Psychology Review* 4(1): 57–75.

MacKinnon, R. (1997) 'Virtual rape', *Journal of Computer-Mediated Communication* (2)4. DOI: 10.1111/j.1083-6101.1997.tb00200.x.

'Man found guilty of sending menacing tweets to Labour MP Stella Creasy' (2014) *The Guardian*, 3 September, available at: http://www.theguardian.com/politics/2014/sep/02/stella-creasy-rape-threats-a-joke (accessed 7/3/16).

Manivannan, V. (2013) 'FCJ-158 Tits or GTFO: The logics of misogyny on 4chan's Random – /b/', *The Fibreculture Journal* 22: 109–132, available at: http://twentytwo.fibreculturejournal.org/fcj-158-tits-or-gtfo-the-logics-of-misogyny-on-4chans-random-b/ (accessed 25/1/16).

Mantilla, K. (2015) *Gendertrolling: How Misogyny Went Viral*. Santa Barbara, CA: Praeger.

Marcetic, B. (2014) '#Gamergate is really about terrorism: Why Bill Maher should be vilifying the gaming community, too', *Salon*, 24 October, available at: http://www.salon.com/2014/10/23/gamergate_is_really_about_terrorism_why_bill_maher_should_be_vilifying_the_gaming_community_too/ (accessed 28/12/15).

Marcotte, A. (2014) 'Anti-feminists are outraged that feminists argue you should only kiss people who are kissing you back', *Raw Story*, 24 June, available at: http://www.rawstory.com/2014/06/anti-feminists-are-outraged-that-feminists-argue-you-should-only-kiss-people-who-are-kissing-you-back/ (accessed 28/12/15).

Marwick, A. (2014) 'Gender, sexuality, and social media', in J. Hunsinger and T. Senft (eds.), *The Social Media Handbook*. New York: Routledge.

Masterson, D. (2006a) 'Germaine Greer is a cunt', *MenAreBetterThanWomen.com*, available at: http://www.menarebetterthanwomen.com/germaine-greer-2/ (accessed 19/10/13).

Masterson, D. (2006b). 'Germaine Greer is a cunt (and a whore). Part II', *Men Are BetterThanWomen.com*, available at: http://www.menarebetterthanwomen.com/germain-greer-is-a-cunt-and-a-whore-part-ii/ (accessed 19/10/13).

Matias, J. N. (2015) 'Common questions about our online harassment report', *MIT Center for Civic Media*, 14 July, available at: https://civic.mit.edu/blog/natematias/common-questions-about-our-online-harassment-report (accessed 20/6/16).

Matias, J. N., Johnson, A., Boesel, W. E., Keegan, B., Friedman, J., and DeTar, C. (2015) 'Reporting, reviewing, and responding to harassment on Twitter', *Women, Action, and the Media*, 13 May, available at: http://womenactionmedia.org/twitter-report (accessed 20/6/16).

Matt, M. (2014) '4chan explains the true meaning of "Tits or GTFO!"', *YouTube*, 17 July, available at: https://www.youtube.com/watch?v=GudcQm8vRb0 (accessed 27/1/16).

Mayer, C. (2013) 'I got a bomb threat on Twitter. Was I right to report it?', *Time*, 2 August, available at: http://world.time.com/2013/08/02/i-got-a-bomb-threat-on-twitter-was-i-right-to-report-it/ (accessed 27/1/16).

Medhora, S. (2016) 'Peter Dutton apologises for calling journalist a "mad witch" in text message', *The Guardian*, 4 January, available at: http://www.theguardian.com/australia-news/2016/jan/04/peter-dutton-apologises-for-calling-journalist-a-mad-witch-in-text-message (accessed 3/2/16).

Mill, J. S. (1863) *On Liberty, 2nd edition*. Boston: Ticknor and Fields.

Millard, A. B. (2015) 'IT HAPPENED TO ME: I posed as a man on Twitter and nobody called me fat or threatened to rape me for once', *xojane*, 26 March, available at: http://www.xojane.com/it-happened-to-me/i-was-a-man-on-twitter?utm_source=huffpost_women&utm_medium=pubexchange (accessed 12/1/16).

Milne, E. (2010) *Letters, Postcards, Email: Technologies of Presence*. New York: Routledge.

Moran, G. (2015) 'This former YouTube exec is taking on internet trolls', *Fastcompany*, 3 September, available at: http://www.fastcompany.com/3050379/this-former-youtube-exec-is-taking-on-internet-trolls (accessed 2/2/16).

Morris, K. (2011) 'The 10 most important people on Reddit in 2011', *The Daily Dot*, 16 December, available at: http://www.dailydot.com/society/daily-dot-top-10-2011-reddit/ (accessed 2/1/16).

Morse, S. J. (2009) 'Addiction, science, and criminal responsibility', in N. A. Farahany (ed.), *The Impact of Behavioral Sciences on Criminal Law*. New York: Oxford University Press.

Moseley, G. L. (2007) *Painful Yarns: Metaphors & Stories to Help Understand the Biology of Pain*. Canberra: Dancing Giraffe Press.

Moseley, G. L. (2011) 'Why things hurt', *TEDxAdelaide*, 21 November, available at: https://www.youtube.com/watch?v=gwd-wLdIHjs (accessed 4/6/16).

Moseley, G. L., Butler, D. S., Beames, T. B., and Giles, T. J. (2012) *The Graded Motor Imagery Handbook*. Adelaide: Noigroup Publications.

Mossberger, K. (2009) 'Toward digital citizenship: Addressing inequality in the information age', in A. Chadwick and P. N. Howard (eds.), *Routledge Handbook of Internet Politics*. New York: Routledge.

Nakamura, L., and Chow-White, P. A. (2012) 'Introduction: Race and digital technology: Code, the color line, and the information society', in L. Nakamura and P. A. Chow-White (eds.), *Race After the Internet*. New York: Routledge.

Naughton, J. (2014) '25 things you might not know about the web on its 25th birthday', *The Guardian*, 9 March, available at: www.theguardian.com/technology/2014/mar/09/25-years-web-tim-berners-lee (accessed 6/4/15).

nochafaa (2015) 'New op idea', *Reddit*, available at: https://www.reddit.com/r/KotakuInAction/comments/3mijmz/new_op_idea/ (accessed 12/1/16).

Noyes, J. (2015) 'Mark Latham admits he was behind the offensive Twitter account that trolled Rosie Batty', *DailyLife*, 16 October, available at: http://www.dailylife.com.au/dl-people/dl-entertainment/mark-latham-admits-he-was-behind-the-offensive-twitter-account-that-trolled-rosie-batty-20151015-gkaj5v.html (accessed 26/4/16).

'NRL cheerleaders to go?' (2009) *AusGamers*, 18 May, available at: http://www.ausgamers.com/forums/news/thread.php/2742772 (accessed 11/12/15).

Nyst, C. (2014) 'End violence: Women's rights and safety online: Internet intermediaries and violence against women online', *Association for Progressive Communications* (APC), July, available at: http://www.genderit.org/sites/default/upload/flow-cnyst-summary-formatted.pdf (accessed 28/1/16).

O'Brien, S. A. (2015) 'This is the year technology hit rock bottom', *CNN Money*, 28 October, available at: http://money.cnn.com/2015/07/19/technology/brianna-wu-reddit-harassment/ (accessed 3/2/16).

O'Doherty, I. (2015) 'People need to toughen up and treat the Twitter trolls with deserved contempt', *Independent.ie*, 29 December, available at: http://www.independent.ie/opinion/columnists/ian-odoherty/people-need-to-toughen-up-and-treat-the-twitter-trolls-with-deserved-contempt-34320055.html (accessed 27/2/16).

Oliphant, V. (2016) '"Vile" Twitter trolls threaten to rape Leicester City striker Jamie Vardy's baby girl', *Express*, 4 April, available at: http://www.express. co.uk/news/uk/658017/Jamie-Vardy-twitter-trolls-threaten-to-rape-daughter (accessed 8/4/16).

O'Neill, B. (2011) 'The campaign to "Stamp Out Misogyny Online" echoes Victorian efforts to protect women from coarse language', *The Telegraph*, 7 November, available at: http://blogs.telegraph.co.uk/news/ brendanoneill2/100115868/the-campaign-to-stamp-out-misogyny-online-echoes-victorian-efforts-to-protect-women-from-coarse-language/ (accessed 28/12/15).

O'Neill, B. (2014) '#Gamergate: We must fight for the right to fantasise', *Spiked*, 8 December, available at: http://www.spiked-online.com/newsite/article/ gamergate-we-must-fight-for-the-right-to-fantasise/16307#.VyExmaN94i4 (accessed 28/4/16).

O'Neill, B. (2015) 'Should people be free to make death threats? Sometimes, yes', *The Spectator*, 3 November, available at: http://blogs.spectator.co.uk/2015/11/ should-people-be-free-to-make-death-threats-sometimes-yes/(accessed 6/1/16).

Oppenheim, M. (2016) 'Labour MP Jess Phillips receives "600 rape threats in one night"', *The Independent*, 1 June, available at: http://www.independent.co.uk/ news/people/labour-mp-jess-phillips-receives-600-rape-threats-in-one-night-a7058041.html (accessed 2/6/16).

O'Sullivan, P. B., and Flanagin, A. J. (2003) 'Reconceptualizing "flaming" and other problematic messages'. *New Media & Society* 5(1). DOI: 10.1177/ 1461444803005001908.

Ostini, J., and Hopkins, S. (2015) 'Online harassment is a form of violence', *The Conversation*, 8 April, available at: https://theconversation.com/online-harassment-is-a-form-of-violence-38846 (accessed 11/1/16).

Patel, N. (2014) 'The internet is fucked (but we can fix it)', *The Verge*, 25 February, available at: http://www.theverge.com/2014/2/25/5431382/the-internet-is-fucked (accessed 26/3/16).

Pariser, E. (2011) *The Filter Bubble: What the Internet Is Hiding from You*. London: Viking.

Pearl, M. (2014) 'This guy's embarrassing relationship drama is killing the 'Gamer' Identity', *Vice*, 29 August, available at: http://www.vice.com/read/ this-guys-embarrassing-relationship-drama-is-killing-the-gamer-identity-828 (accessed 28/12/15).

Penny, L. (2011) 'Laurie Penny: A woman's opinion is the mini-skirt of the internet', *Independent*, 4 November, available at: http://www.independent. co.uk/voices/commentators/laurie-penny-a-womans-opinion-is-the-mini-skirt-of-the-internet-6256946.html (accessed 23/12/15).

Philipson, A. (2013) 'Woman who campaigned for Jane Austen bank note receives Twitter death threats', *The Telegraph*, 28 July, available at: http:// www.telegraph.co.uk/technology/10207231/Womanwho-campaigned-for-Jane-Austen-bank-note-receives-Twitter-death-threats.html (accessed 14/6/16).

Phillips, W. (2011) 'LOLing at tragedy: Facebook trolls, memorial pages and resistance to grief online'. *First Monday* 16 (12), 5 December, available at: http://firstmonday.org/ojs/index.php/fm/article/view/3168 (accessed 24/12/13).

Phillips, W. (2013) 'Don't feed the trolls? It's not that simple', *The Daily Dot*, 10 June, available at: http://www.dailydot.com/opinion/phillips-dont-feed-trolls-antisocial-web/ (accessed 18/3/16).

Phillips, W. (2015a) *This Is Why We Can't Have Nice Things: Mapping the Relationship Between Online Trolling and Mainstream Culture.* Cambridge, MA: MIT Press.

Phillips, W. (2015b) 'We're the reason we can't have nice things on the internet', *Quartz*, 29 December, available at: http://qz.com/582113/were-the-reason-we-cant-have-nice-things-online/ (accessed 31/12/15).

Phillips, W. (2015c) 'Let's call "trolling" what it really is', *The Kernel*, 10 May, available at: http://kernelmag.dailydot.com/issue-sections/staff-editorials/12898/trolling-stem-tech-sexism/ (accessed 7/2/16).

Phipps, A. (2014) 'The dark side of the impact agenda', *The Times Higher Education*, 4 December, available at: https://www.timeshighereducation.com/comment/opinion/the-dark-side-of-the-impact-agenda/2017299.article (accessed 16/3/16).

Plunkett, L. (2012) 'Awful things happen when you try to make a video about video game stereotypes', *Kotaku*, 12 June, available at: http://www.kotaku.com/5917623/awful-things-happenwhen-you-try-to-make-a-video-about-video-game-stereotypes (accessed 28/12/15).

'Police workforce, England and Wales: 31 March 2015' (2015), *gov.uk*, 16 July, available at: https://www.gov.uk/government/publications/police-workforce-england-and-wales-31-march-2015/police-workforce-england-and-wales-31-march-2015 (accessed 1/5/16).

Postmes, T., Spears, R., and Lea, M. (2000) 'The formation of group norms in computer-mediated communication', *Human Communication Research* 26(3): 341–371. DOI: 10.1111/j.1468-2958.2000.tb00761.x.

Powell, A., and Henry, N. (2015a) 'Digital harassment and abuse of adult Australians: A summary report', *Tech & Me Project*, RMIT University, available at: https://research.techandme.com.au/wp-content/uploads/REPORT_AustraliansExperiencesofDigitalHarassmentandAbuse.pdf (accessed 19/6/16).

Powell, A., and Henry, N. (2015b) 'How can we stem the tide of online harassment and abuse?', *The Conversation*, 5 October, available at: https://theconversation.com/how-can-we-stem-the-tide-of-online-harassment-and-abuse-48387 (accessed 12/5/16).

Price, M. (2016) 'The feminist cupcake sale that led to death and rape threats', *The Guardian*, 6 April, available at: http://www.theguardian.com/commentisfree/2016/apr/06/the-feminist-cupcake-sale-that-led-us-into-the-darkest-depths-of-gender-inequality (accessed 15/4/16).

Rahman, S. (2015) 'Biased cyberhate researcher: My response', *In Pursuit of Rational Thought*, 29 June, available at:https://saraarahman.wordpress.com/2015/06/29/biased-cyberhate-researcher-my-response/ (accessed 2/1/16).

Randol, E. F. (2005) 'Homeland security and the co-optation of feminist discourse', in S. M. Meagher and P. DiQuinzio (eds.), *Women and Children First: Feminism, Rhetoric, and Public Policy*. Albany: State University of New York.

Riley, D. (2015) 'Bad idea: Why Google shouldn't be involved in removing revenge porn on its own volition', *Silicon Angle*, 23 June, available at: http://siliconangle.com/blog/2015/06/23/bad-idea-why-google-shouldnt-be-involved-in-removing-revenge-porn-on-its-own-volition/ (accessed 12/5/16).

Roberts, J. V., Stalans, L. J., Indermaur, D., and Hough, M. (2003) *Penal Populism and Public Opinion: Lessons from Five Countries*. Oxford: Oxford University Press.

Robertson A. (2014). 'Gamergate can't stop being about harassment', *The Verge*, 23 October, available at: http://www.theverge.com/2014/10/23/7047647/felicia-day-response-shows-why-good-gamergate-is-still-hurting-people (accessed 20/6/16).

Roy, J. (2015) 'If you don't take online harassment seriously, "Congratulations on your white penis"', *The Cut*, 22 June, available at: http://nymag.com/thecut/2015/06/john-oliver-takes-on-online-harassment-of-women.html (accessed 3/1/16).

Sabin, S. (2015) 'For some tech feminists, online harassment is a constant', *CNBC*, 19 August, available at: http://www.cnbc.com/2015/08/19/for-some-tech-feminists-online-harassment-is-a-constant.html (accessed 17/5/16).

Sainty, L. (2015) 'A woman has been banned from Facebook after sharing the abusive messages she was sent by men', *BuzzFeed*, 21 June, available at: http://www.buzzfeed.com/lanesainty/a-woman-has-been-banned-from-facebook-after-sharing-the-abus#.mf60NrekkN (accessed 2/2/16).

Sandoval, G. (2013) 'The end of kindness: Weev and the cult of the angry young man', *The Verge*, 12 September, available at: http://www.theverge.com/2013/9/12/4693710/the-end-of-kindness-weev-and-the-cult-of-the-angry-young-man (accessed 22/12/15).

Sarkeesian, A. (2012a) 'Harassment, misogyny and silencing on YouTube', *Feminist Frequency*, 7 June, available at: http://www.feministfrequency.com/2012/06/harassment-misogyny-and-silencing-on-youtube/ (accessed 18/12/15).

Sarkeesian, A. (2012b) 'Image based harassment and visual misogyny', *Feminist Frequency*, 1 July, available at: http://feministfrequency.com/2012/07/01/image-based-harassment-and-visual-misogyny/ (accessed 28/12/15).

Sarkeesian, A. (2015a) 'Talking publicly about harassment generates more harassment', *Feminist Frequency*, 29 October, available at http://feministfrequency.com/2015/10/29/talking-publicly-about-harassment-generates-more-harassment/#more-34166 (accessed 30/11/15).

Sarkeesian, A. (2015b) 'Women as reward', *Feminist Frequency*, 31 August, available at: http://feministfrequency.com/2015/08/31/women-as-reward/ (accessed 3/2/16).

Schwartz, M. (2008) 'The trolls among us', *The New York Times Magazine*, 3 August, available at: http://www.nytimes.com/2008/08/03/magazine/03trolls-t.html?pagewanted=all&_r=0 (accessed 26/2/16).

Sierra, K. (2014) 'Why the trolls will always win', *Wired*, 8 October, available at: http://www.wired.com/2014/10/trolls-will-always-win/ (accessed 22/12/15).

Singal, J. (2014) 'Gamergate should stop lying to journalists – and itself', *Science of Us*, 20 October, available at: http://nymag.com/scienceofus/2014/10/gamergate-should-stop-lying-to-itself.html# (accessed 29/12/15).

Slater, D. (2002) 'Social relationships and identity online and offline', in L. A. Lievrouw and S. Livingstone (eds.), *Handbook of New Media: Social Shaping and Consequences of ICTs*. London: Sage.

Sproull, L. and Kiesler, S. (1986) 'Reducing social context cues: Electronic mail in organizational communication'. *Management Science* 32(11): 1492–1512.

StilRH (2014) *Reddit*, available at: https://www.reddit.com/r/4chan/comments/1ppdvf/tits_or_gtfo/ (accessed 27/1/16).

Smith, L. (2014) 'Domestic violence and online abuse: Half UK survivors experience trolling in "tidal wave of hate"', *International Business Times*, 1 March, available at: http://www.ibtimes.co.uk/domestic-violence-online-abuse-half-uk-survivors-experience-trolling-tidal-wave-hate-1438420 (accessed 7/1/16).

Smith, L. (2016) 'International Women's Day 2016: Ten facts, figures and statistics about women's rights', *International Business Times*, 8 March, available at: http://www.ibtimes.co.uk/international-womens-day-2016-ten-facts-figures-statistics-about-womens-rights-1548083 (accessed 15/4/16).

Stevens, J. (2013) 'Our town's like a foreign country and locals can't cope with the immigrants, says mother after TV clash with academic on Question Time', *Daily Mail Australia*, 19 January, available at: http://www.dailymail.co.uk/news/article-2264799/Our-towns-like-foreign-country-Locals-cope-immigrants-says-mother-TV-clash-academic.html?ito=feeds-newsxml (accessed 27/2/16).

Stone, T. (2013a) 'Tyler the Creator shouldn't be allowed to verbally abuse me', *The Guardian*, 7 June, available at: http://www.theguardian.com/commentisfree/2013/jun/07/tyler-the-creator-rape-abuse (accessed 7/1/16).

Stone, T. (2013b) 'US Rapper Tyler the Creator unleashes a torrent of hate on Sydney activist', *Melinda Tankard Reist* (originally published in *Daily Life*), 7 August, available at: http://melindatankardreist.com/2013/08/why-im-calling-on-twitter-to-stop-abuse/ (accessed 23/6/16).

Stryker, C. (2011) *Epic Win for Anonymous: How 4chan's Army Conquered the Web*. New York: Overlook Duckworth.

Stuart, K. (2014a) 'Brianna Wu and the human cost of Gamergate: "Every woman I know in the industry is scared"', *The Guardian*, 18 October, available at: http://www.theguardian.com/technology/2014/oct/17/brianna-wu-gamergate-human-cost (accessed 28/12/15).

Stuart, K. (2014b) 'Zoe Quinn: "All Gamergate has done is ruin people's lives"', *The Guardian*, 4 December, available at: http://www.theguardian.com/technology/2014/dec/03/zoe-quinn-gamergate-interview (accessed 22/12/15).

Summers, A. (1994 [1975]) *Damned Whores and God's Police: The Colonisation of Women in Australia*. Victoria: Penguin Books.

Taylor, M. (2016) 'Chiropractor denies racially attacking Senator Nova Peris on Facebook', *Herald Sun*, May 29, available at:http://www.heraldsun.com.au/

news/chiropractor-denies-racially-attacking-senator-nova-peris-on-facebook/
news-story/c86f0bc59fff9bf6f0c937405affd9d9 (accessed 2/6/16).

'The 43rd Parliament: Traits and trends' (2013) Parliament of Australia, 2 October, available at: http://www.aph.gov.au/About_Parliament/Parliamentary_Departments/Parliamentary_Library/pubs/rp/rp1314/43rdParl (accessed 28/1/16).

'The state of broadband 2015' (2015) The Broadband Commission for Digital Development, United Nations Educational, Scientific and Cultural Organization, September, available at: http://www.broadbandcommission.org/documents/reports/bb-annualreport2015.pdf (accessed 28/1/16).

'The use of misogynistic terms on Twitter' (2016) *Demos*, available at: http://www.demos.co.uk/wp-content/uploads/2016/05/Misogyny-online.pdf (accessed 16/6/16)

Thériault, A. (2015) 'Let's call female online harassment what it really is: Terrorism', *Vice*, 13 February, available at: http://www.vice.com/read/lets-call-female-online-harassment-what-it-really-is-gender-terrorism-481 (accessed 3/1/16).

Thompsen, P. A., and Foulger, D. A. (1996) 'Effects of pictographs and quoting on flaming in electronic mail', *Computers in Human Behavior* 12(2): 225–243.

Thomson, C. J. (2012) 'Celebrities vs. Twitter trolls: Why walking away is better than involving politicians & the law.' *WordswithMeaning!*, 10 September, available at: http://www.wordswithmeaning.org/celebrities-vs-twitter-trolls-why-walking-away-is-better-than-involving-polticians-the-law/#axzz2Hu2JPbR1 (accessed 10/10/12).

Thorpe, V. and Rogers, R. (2011) 'Women bloggers call for a stop to "hateful" trolling by misogynist men', *The Guardian*, 6 November, available at: http://www.theguardian.com/world/2011/nov/05/women-bloggers-hateful-trolling (accessed 14/4/16).

Tiku, N., and Newton, C. (2015) 'Twitter CEO: "We suck at dealing with abuse"', *The Verge*, 4 February, available at: http://www.theverge.com/2015/2/4/7982099/twitter-ceo-sent-memo-taking-personal-responsibility-for-the (accessed 3/1/16).

'Trusty Support' (n.d.) Available at: https://twitter.com/trustysupport (accessed 1/5/16).

Turnage, A. K. (2008) 'Email flaming behaviors and organizational conflict', *Journal of Computer-Mediated Communication* 13: 43–59. DOI: 10.1111/j.1083-6101.2007.00385.x.

Unknown (2015) 'Reddit in 2015', *Reddit Blog*, 31 December, available at: http://www.redditblog.com/2015/12/reddit-in-2015.html (accessed 2/1/16).

Valenti, J. (2016) 'Insults and rape threats: Writers shouldn't have to deal with this', *The Guardian*, 15 April, available at: http://www.theguardian.com/commentisfree/2016/apr/14/insults-rape-threats-writers-online-harassment (accessed 15/4/16).

Van den Hoven, J. (2013) 'Value sensitive design and responsible innovation', in R. Owen, J. Bessant, and M. Heintz (eds.), *Responsible Innovation: Managing the Responsible Emergence of Science and Innovation in Society*. Chichester: John Wiley & Sons.

Van Deursen, A. J. A. M., and Van Dijk, J. A. G. M. (2014) 'The digital divide shifts to differences in usage', *New Media & Society* 16(3): 507–526.

Van Dijk, J., and Hacker, K. (2003) 'The digital divide as a complex and dynamic phenomenon', *The Information Society* 19(4): 315–326.

Van Mill, D. (2015) 'Freedom of speech', in E. N. Zalta (ed.), *The Stanford Encyclopedia of Philosophy*, available at: http://plato.stanford.edu/archives/spr2015/entries/freedom-speech/ (accessed 3/6/16).

Vernon, J. (2016) 'Zane Alchin pleads guilty to making Facebook threats about Olivia Melville Tinder profile', *abc.net.au*, 20 June, available at: http://mobile.abc.net.au/news/2016-06-20/zane-alchin-pleads-guilty-to-facebook-abuse-of-olivia-melville/7525664?pfm=sm&section=nsw (accessed 20/6/16).

Vrooman, S. S. (2002) 'The art of invective: Performing identity in cyberspace', *New Media & Society* 4(1): 51–70.

Walsh, J. (2007) 'Men who hate women on the web: And the women (like me) who try to ignore them. Or at least I did – until the Kathy Sierra affair', *Salon*, 1 April, available at: http://www.salon.com/2007/03/31/sierra/ (accessed 22/12/15).

Walters, M., and Tumath, J. (2014) 'Gender "hostility", rape, and the hate crime paradigm', *The Modern Law Review* 77(4): 563–596.

Wang, H. (1996) 'Flaming: More than a necessary evil for academic mailing lists', *The Electronic Journal of Communication* 6(1).

'Web Index: Report 2014–15' (n.d.), *Web Index*, available at: http://thewebindex.org/wp-content/uploads/2014/12/Web_Index_24pp_November2014.pdf (accessed 29/6/16).

Wertheimer, A. (1987) *Coercion*. Princeton: Princeton University Press.

West, L (2013a) 'If comedy has no lady problem, why am I getting so many rape threats?', *Jezebel*, 6 April, available at: http://www.jezebel.com/if-comedy-has-no-lady-problem-why-am-i-getting-so-many-511214385 (accessed 27/12/15).

West, L. (2013b) 'Don't ignore the trolls: Feed them until they explode', *Jezebel*, 31 July, available at: http://jezebel.com/dont-ignore-the-trolls-feed-them-until-they-explode-977453815 (accessed 13/3/16).

West, L. (2015) 'What happened when I confronted my cruellest troll', *The Guardian*, 3 February, available at: http://www.theguardian.com/society/2015/feb/02/what-happened-confronted-cruellest-troll-lindy-west (accessed 3/2/16).

West, P. (2015) 'Stop taking Twitter death threats seriously', *Spiked*, 22 April, available at: http://www.spiked-online.com/newsite/article/stop-taking-twitter-death-threats-seriously/16895#.Vo7tgZN97Yp (accessed 8/1/16).

Wheeler, D. L. (2011) 'Does the internet empower? A look at the internet and international development', in M. Consalvo and C. Ess (eds.), *The Handbook of Internet Studies*. West Sussex: Wiley-Blackwell.

Wilson, J., McCrea, C., and Fuller, G. (2012) 'CFP: Special Issue: The politics of trolling and the negative space of the internet', *The Fibreculture Journal*, available at: http://fibreculturejournal.org/cfp-special-issue-for-the-fibreculture-journal-the-politics-of-trolling-and-the-negative-space-of-the-internet/ (accessed 13/1/13).

Wimsatt, W. K., and Beardsley, M. C. (1946) 'The intentional fallacy', *The Sewanee Review*, 54(3): 468–488.

Wittes, B., Poplin, C., Jurecic, Q., and Spera, C. (2016) 'Sextortion: Cybersecurity, teenagers, and remote sexual assault', *Brookings Institution*, May, available at: https://www.brookings.edu/wp-content/uploads/2016/05/sextortion1-1.pdf

Wohling, T. (2015), 'WAM! Bam! Narrative dead!', *TechRaptor*, 23 May, available at: http://techraptor.net/content/wam-bam-narrative-dead (accessed 20/6/16).

Yaffe, G. (2003) 'Indoctrination, coercion, and freedom of will', *Yale Law School*, Faculty Scholarship Series Paper 3726, available at: http://digitalcommons. law.yale.edu/fss_papers/3726 (accessed 13/1/16).

'You play video games? So are you fat, ugly or slutty?', *Fat, Ugly or Slutty*, available at: fatuglyorslutty.com (accessed 2/5/16).

Young, C. (2015a) 'The pecking disorder: Social justice warriors gone wild', *Observer*, 11 June, available at: http://observer.com/2015/06/the-pecking-disorder-social-justice-warriors-gone-wild/ (accessed 29/12/15).

Young, C. (2015b) 'Blame GamerGate's bad rep on smears and shoddy journalism', *Observer*, 13 October, available at: http://observer.com/2015/10/blame-gamergates-bad-rep-on-smears-and-shoddy-journalism/ (accessed 28/12/15).

INDEX

doxing 4, 56–7, 59
  and moving home 63, 64
  and silencing 69–70
Doyle, Sady 2, 16, 36, 40–1, 67

Elam, Paul 2
Electronic Frontier Foundation (EFF) 116
Elliot, Amanda 67–8
Elliot, Cath 81–2
embodied responses 65–6
employment, losses and future
    prospects 66–8
ex-partners 29–32, 57–60, 91
  see also revenge porn
exclusion
  of female gamers 99–100
  Get The Fuck Out (GTFO) 1, 46–9
excuse-making 80–5
  institutional responses 107–10

Facebook 57–8, 59–60, 81–2, 90–1, 92, 95
Farah, Robbie 11
Farrow, Caroline 27
Fat, Ugly or Slutty (website) 40
Fat Heffalump (blog) 53–4
Federal Bureau of Investigations (FBI) 60,
    89, 90
feminist journalism, letter and email
    responses compared 18–20, 23–4
feminist perspective 114–17
feminist vigilantism 62
Filipovic, Jill 71
'filter bubble' 51
financial costs 66–8
Fish, S.E. 109–10
'flaming' 101–2, 103, 104, 105
  authorial intention 82–4
Ford, Clementine 1, 95
4chan 30–1, 36, 46–8, 49–50, 51
Frazelle, Jessie 97–8
free speech defense 55, 77, 108,
    109–10, 116
Funnell, Nina 26–7

Gale, Julie 27
Gamergate 3, 13–14, 28–34, 64, 67–8,
    69–70, 89–90
  and Reddit 107
  and scholarly research 100–1

Gamergate cont.
  South by Southwest (SXSW)
    harassment threats 99
gamers
  and fan cultures 98–100
  gender-swapping/male avatars
    17–18, 71
  gaming industry responses 97–100
Gardiner, et al. 17
gender inequities 43–4, 46–9, 94
gender stereotyping 27–8, 98
Get The Fuck Out (GTFO) 1, 46–9
  and exclusion of female gamers
    99–100
Gjoni, Eron 29–30
Goldberg, M. 44, 61, 69, 71
'Google bombing' 29
grammatical/spelling errors 102
group dynamics 22
The Guardian 17

Hardaker, Claire 32–3
harms: embodied responses 65–6
Henry, N. and Powell, A./Powell, A. and
    Henry, N. 17, 23, 58, 59, 65, 95
Hermida, Alfred 102
Hess, A. 61, 64, 68, 71, 88–9, 116

'image macros' 50
image-based harassment 29, 57, 58
inside information 12–13
institutional responses
  excuse-making 107–10
  gaming industry 97–100
  police 4, 36–40, 80–1, 88–92
  policy-makers 92–5
  scholarship 100–7
  social media platforms 95–7
intention, authorial 82–4

Jackman, C. 26–7
Jane, E.A. 2, 11, 62, 101, 102, 105
Jason, Z. 3, 29, 30–1, 90, 95
joking defense 81–2, 85
Judd, Ashley 41

Kluwe, Chris 70
Kratz, Ken 11
Krotoski, Aleks 46